Edge Computing Patterns for Solution Architects

Learn methods and principles of resilient distributed application architectures from hybrid cloud to far edge

Ashok Iyengar and Joseph Pearson

Edge Computing Patterns for Solution Architects

Group Product Manager: Kunal Sawant
Publishing Product Manager: Samriddhi Murarka
Book Project Manager: Manisha Singh
Senior Editor: Nithya Sadanandan
Technical Editor: Vidhisha Patidar
Copy Editor: Safis Editing
Indexer: Pratik Shirodkar
Production Designer: Ponraj Dhandapani
DevRel Marketing Coordinator: Shrinidhi Manoharan
Business Development Executive: Debadrita Chatterjee

First published: January 2024

Production reference: 1190124

Published by Packt Publishing Ltd.
Grosvenor House
11 St Paul's Square
Birmingham
B3 1RB, UK

ISBN 978-1-80512-406-1

www.packtpub.com

This book would not be possible without the unwavering support and understanding of Radha and tons of encouragement from Sameer, Siddharth, and Mythili. They collectively inspire me with their own successes. And to my newest cheerleader, Seelan, who never ceases to amaze me.

-- Ashok Iyengar

To my mentor and guide, Rob High. Thanks for the guidance, trust, and opportunity to learn about edge computing.

– Joe Pearson

Contributors

About the authors

Ashok Iyengar is an Executive Cloud Architect at IBM. As a member of the Architecture Guild, he focuses on creating solution architectures that encompass distributed computing, edge computing and AI. He follows NDSU Bison football and is eagerly looking forward to bringing generative AI to edge computing. He enjoys being a mentor, author, speaker and blogger.

I owe a debt of gratitude to my co-author, Joe Pearson, who keeps me honest. I would not have undertaken this effort if it was not for his willingness, encouragement and tireless work ethic.

Joseph Pearson has worked as a college instructor and in various media companies for over three decades, most recently as Software Architect at The Weather Channel on weather.com. He has since worked for IBM Cloud as a Strategist and then IBM Software in Edge Computing. He currently works for IBM Software's Networking and Edge Computing unit on their open source strategy. He volunteers with the Linux Foundation as Chair of the LF Edge **Technical Advisory Council** (TAC) and leads the Open Horizon project. And in any spare time, he enjoys geocaching.

I would like to thank my wife and children for bearing with me as I stole time from them throughout the process of writing this book. I especially want to thank Ashok Iyengar for supporting and encouraging me to tackle working on this book when it seemed so daunting. It's always helpful to have an experienced friend and author to collaborate with who can also be a big brother and provide frank guidance when it's most needed.

About the reviewer

Frédéric Desbiens manages Embedded, IoT, and Edge Computing programs at the Eclipse Foundation, Europe's largest open-source organization. His job is to help the community innovate by bringing devices and software together. He is a strong supporter of open source. In the past, he worked as a product manager, solutions architect, and developer for companies as diverse as Pivotal, Cisco, and Oracle. Frédéric holds an MBA in electronic commerce, a BASc in Computer Science, and a BEd, all from Université Laval (Québec City, Canada).

Frédéric is the author of "Building Enterprise IoT Solutions using Eclipse IoT Technologies: An Open-Source Approach to Edge Computing," published in December 2022 by Apress (ISBN: 978-1484288818).

Table of Contents

Part 2: Solution Architecture Archetypes in Context

3

Core Edge Architecture   41

4

Network Edge Architecture   59

Part 3: Related Considerations and Concluding Thoughts

6

Data Has Weight and Inertia   95

7

Automate to Achieve Scale   111

8

Monitoring and Observability   127

9

Connect Judiciously but Thoughtlessly   139

10

Open Source Software Can Benefit You   155

11

Recommendations and Best Practices   169

Preface

Edge computing as we know it has rapidly evolved from its early days as a successor to the **Internet of Things (IoT)**. Processing data at the source has become the ultimate goal because businesses and people expect analytics insights to be available and transaction results to be cleared in real time. That includes medical analysis, money transfers, payment receipts, video inferencing, and voice recognition. All this is possible because devices have become "smart" and the communication networks are able to deliver high speed and high throughput with low latencies to these new deployments. We have seen the rise of a new paradigm of application architecture specifically designed to run in domains that are not only constrained but also widely distributed. The IT architectures facilitating these advancements are unique because of the very nature of edge computing.

If the name of the game is to get insights quickly from all the data, we have to ensure there are applications able to do that, devices that can host the applications, and a network facilitating the information flow. That is the challenge solution architects face, which is who this book is primarily written for.

Drawing from real-world deployments in large enterprises and standards proposed by edge computing community organizations, this book emphasizes practical and tested-at-scale patterns and best practices used by leading companies worldwide. The book takes the reader from edge computing terminology and concepts to simple architectures, and eventually through end-to-end industry-specific approaches. It gives several points of view and rules of thumb and provides resources and recommendations for deeper thinking and research.

Who this book is for

This book is intended for IT professionals who have created solution architectures and are looking to extend their skills to the edge computing space. It should be valuable to VPs of IT infrastructure, enterprise architects, solution architects, and SRE professionals who are familiar with cloud computing and are interested in creating an edge reference architecture or a solution architecture for a particular industry use case. The book provides common patterns from solutions implemented by customers in industries ranging from retail to telcos to manufacturing.

What this book covers

Chapter 1, Our View of Edge Computing, establishes a shared vernacular, describes infrastructure scenarios, and relies on industry conventions to ensure standard and widely compatible solutions.

Chapter 2, Edge Architectural Components, covers four roles of components in edge architectures, benefits and limitations, and functional versus non-functional requirements.

Chapter 3, Core Edge Architecture, covers managing and enabling sensors and smart devices using the Edge Device Hub pattern.

Chapter 4, Network Edge Architecture, explores transitioning to software-defined network architectures to enable digital service provider scenarios.

Chapter 5, End-to-End Edge Architecture, brings together devices, macro components, and applications to solve industry-specific challenges.

Chapter 6, Data Has Weight and Inertia, explores the data-related considerations that edge-native solutions will need to address.

Chapter 7, Automate to Achieve Scale, includes approaches that have worked at the extreme scales that edge deployments may encounter.

Chapter 8, Monitoring and Observability, covers how to ensure that a deployed edge solution is performing as designed, despite unique challenges.

Chapter 9, Connect Judiciously but Thoughtlessly, covers three connection scenarios and how application-centered approaches can address them.

Chapter 10, Open Source Software Can Benefit You, explores strategies for ensuring that open source dependencies are used optimally, and when and how an enterprise should open source their solutions.

Chapter 11, Recommendations and Best Practices, takes a wider view of the problem space and how thinking deeply about what you are doing and why can yield some surprising insights.

Images used in the book

You can find the images used in this book in the GitHub repository at `https://github.com/PacktPublishing/Edge-Computing-Patterns-for-Solution-Architects`.

Conventions used

There are a number of text conventions used throughout this book.

`Code in text`: Indicates code words in text, database table names, folder names, filenames, file extensions, pathnames, dummy URLs, user input, and Twitter handles. Here is an example: "If you notice closely, it is an Open Horizon environment variable, namely `HZN_DEVICE_ID`."

A block of code is set as follows:

```
#!/bin/sh
# Simple edge service
while true; do
    echo "HZN_DEVICE_ID says: Hello from Packt!"
    sleep 5
done
```

Bold: Indicates a new term, an important word, or words that you see onscreen. For instance, words in menus or dialog boxes appear in **bold**. Here is an example: "The following code snippet is a very simple Hello World service that outputs **Hello from Packt** every five seconds."

> **Tips or important notes**
> Appear like this.

Get in touch

Feedback from our readers is always welcome.

General feedback: If you have questions about any aspect of this book, email us at `customercare@packtpub.com` and mention the book title in the subject of your message.

Errata: Although we have taken every care to ensure the accuracy of our content, mistakes do happen. If you have found a mistake in this book, we would be grateful if you would report this to us. Please visit `www.packtpub.com/support/errata` and fill in the form.

Piracy: If you come across any illegal copies of our works in any form on the internet, we would be grateful if you would provide us with the location address or website name. Please contact us at `copyright@packt.com` with a link to the material.

If you are interested in becoming an author: If there is a topic that you have expertise in and you are interested in either writing or contributing to a book, please visit `authors.packtpub.com`.

Share Your Thoughts

Once you've read *Edge Computing Patterns for Solution Architects*, we'd love to hear your thoughts! Scan the QR code below to go straight to the Amazon review page for this book and share your feedback.

https://packt.link/r/1805124064

Your review is important to us and the tech community and will help us make sure we're delivering excellent quality content.

Download a free PDF copy of this book

Thanks for purchasing this book!

Do you like to read on the go but are unable to carry your print books everywhere?

Is your eBook purchase not compatible with the device of your choice?

Don't worry, now with every Packt book you get a DRM-free PDF version of that book at no cost.

Read anywhere, any place, on any device. Search, copy, and paste code from your favorite technical books directly into your application.

The perks don't stop there, you can get exclusive access to discounts, newsletters, and great free content in your inbox daily

Follow these simple steps to get the benefits:

1. Scan the QR code or visit the link below

https://packt.link/free-ebook/9781805124061

2. Submit your proof of purchase
3. That's it! We'll send your free PDF and other benefits to your email directly

Part 1: Overview of Edge Computing as a Problem Space

To build a shared understanding, we lay the groundwork and survey the territory in the first two chapters. Since the concepts and terminology in edge computing can be overloading, it's important to explain exactly what is meant when we elucidate our concepts, problems, and solutions. The first two chapters in the book aim to provide clarity and a common foundation that will be built on in Parts 2 and 3. This part begins with how to think and talk about edge computing grounded in context. It then delves into the various components, describes their purposes, and shows how they relate to others and where they best fit.

This part has the following chapters:

- *Chapter 1, Our View of Edge Computing*
- *Chapter 2, Edge Architectural Components*

1

Our View of Edge Computing

One of the first challenges when discussing edge computing between IT professionals is establishing a shared vernacular. In the authors' experience, professionals in this space differ in how they describe the goals, methods, available tools, and deployment targets/operating environments. We've also found that, due to experiences and even generational distinctions, some fundamental assumptions may be at play. By agreeing on a definition of terms at the outset, we avoid misunderstandings and talking past each other.

In this chapter, we will start by describing various edge computing scenarios from an infrastructure point of view, moving from cloud to far edge based on our experiences, research, and available de facto standards. Along the way, we compare and contrast different points of view that will affect architectural choices you can make, such as edge computing versus distributed computing and the network edge versus the enterprise edge.

We will rely on conventions covered in the *Suggested pre-reading material* section, such as *State of the Edge* annual reports and *LF Edge* whitepapers. By the end of the chapter, you should have the shared vocabulary and a wider perspective needed to engage in fruitful conversations on edge computing with software architects and other IT professionals.

In this chapter, we will cover the following main topics:

- Speaking like an edge native
- Which edge? Categorizing edges
- Your computer or mine? Tactics for service deployment
- Cloud-out versus edge-in
- Introducing archetype patterns

Suggested pre-reading material

- *State of the Edge Report 2023* (*The Linux Foundation*)

  (`https://stateoftheedge.com/reports/state-of-the-edge-report-2023/`)

- *From DevOps to EdgeOps: A Vision for Edge Computing* (*Eclipse Foundation*) (`https://outreach.eclipse.foundation/edge-computing-edgeops-white-paper`)

- *Sharpening the Edge – Part 1* (*LF Edge*) (`https://lfedge.org/wp-content/uploads/sites/24/2023/12/LFEdge_Akraino_Whitepaper2_v1_PrePrint.pdf`)

- *Sharpening the Edge – Part 2* (*LF Edge*) (`https://lfedge.org/wp-content/uploads/sites/24/2023/12/LFEdgeTaxonomyWhitepaper_062222.pdf`)

- *Software-as-a-Service (SaaS) overview* (`https://www.salesforce.com/saas/`)

- *Defining software deployment as days* (`https://dzone.com/articles/defining-day-2-operations`)

Speaking like an edge native

In this section, you will learn to articulate fundamental differences between the edge and the cloud. This impacts the available infrastructure, platforms, services, and application deployments. Additionally, you will be able to explain concisely what the edge is and what the field of edge computing does to both **line-of-business** (**LOB**) executives and other non-IT professionals. This includes being able to explain the value it can provide, as well as why this field is emerging at this point in time.

What is the edge?

The *edge* in edge computing is commonly used to describe *the location where computing takes place*. The name itself is meant to evoke a spot in a corner or by the wayside, and not in a central area, and actually refers to the very end of a communications network (the edge of the internet; see *Figure 1.1*). Thus, edge computing happens *outside* a cloud computing facility, and many times outside the four walls of a traditional **data center** (**DC**).

Edge computing describes computing capabilities situated at degrees of distance from a centralized location, usually the cloud or a corporate DC. The placement of the equipment is chosen in order to improve the performance, security, and operating cost of the applications and services that will run in that environment. In exchange, some factors may be de-emphasized, such as resilience, availability, and throughput. Edge computing can reduce latency and bandwidth constraints of services by not transferring collected data to the cloud or a DC for processing and thus not needing to remotely retrieve subsequently generated information. Most recently, the edge has also become a frequent deployment target for control logic supporting industrial automation and **machine learning** (**ML**) models used in visual analytics tasks.

By shortening the distance between devices and the computational resources that serve them, the edge brings new value to existing use cases and can introduce new classes of applications. This results in distributing workloads and ML assets southbound along the path between today's centralized DCs and the increasingly large number of deployed edge computing devices and clusters in the field, on both the **service provider** (**SP**) and user sides of the last mile network – the portion of the SP network that reaches user premises.

> **Note**
>
> When the terms "southbound" and "northbound" are used when discussing an application architecture, they refer to points of the compass in reference to the relative location of your current point of view. So, "northbound" would refer to services, tiers, and locations that are more physically proximate to the cloud, or, in the case of *Figure 1.1*, locations to the right-hand side. Likewise, "southbound" refers to locations closer to the user edge, or locations on the left-hand side.

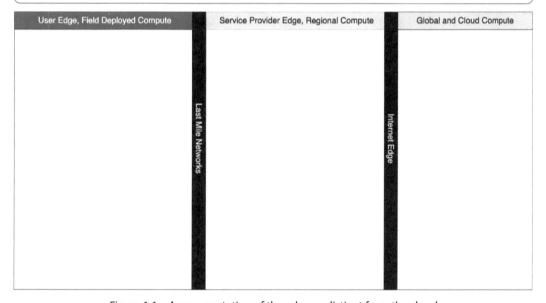

Figure 1.1 – A representation of the edge as distinct from the cloud

Notice in the preceding diagram, which we will be using as a starting point for many charts used throughout the book, how all computing resources located to the left of the thick, black line labeled **Internet Edge** would be considered the edge, and all computing resources to the right of the line would be considered the cloud. Despite those designations, you might hear about "clouds" located in the SP edge referred to as "regional clouds" or "enterprise clouds" and in the user edge as "edge clouds." Future iterations of the chart will collapse the **Internet Edge** and **Last Mile Networks** lines.

Edge computing, therefore, is described by ways in which its operating environments are different than the physical security, hardware homogeneity, and service scalability of cloud computing. Edge compute nodes (and by *nodes*, we include both standalone devices and compute clusters) can be solitary, and many times are not rack-mounted. Edge nodes may not have reliable or consistent power, network connectivity, or even air filtering, climate control, and controlled physical access. Multiplicities of edge nodes may not be the same version or brand of hardware, with differing specifications and capacities, and thus edge computing nodes are described as heterogeneous. Edge nodes may use smaller or fewer processors, slower and/or more power-efficient processors, and fewer specialty or co-processors to accelerate specific types of tasks or workloads. Last, edge nodes may have a permanent or fixed placement or might have mobility or otherwise be portable.

Moving on to the contents of edge nodes … the type of chip being used, the micro-architecture, could be mounted in a constrained device or an off-the-shelf, commodity unit, but it typically runs a Linux distribution or similar enterprise- or consumer-class operating system. We do not speak of embedded systems or fixed-function devices of the IoT class as being used for edge computing functions, although they certainly are used to send data northbound to edge computing systems.

> **Edge micro-architectures**
>
> Typical chip micro-architectures supported by most edge computing solutions include:
>
> - `x86_64 or amd64`
>
> - `arm32 or arm6, arm7`
>
> - `arm64 or armhf, including Apple M1 and M2`
>
> - `ppc64le`
>
> - `risc-v`
>
> - `s390x` (typically running LinuxONE)

When writing and packaging applications for the edge, we no longer write an application in a high-level language such as Python, NodeJS, or even Golang, and package it up for a package delivery system such as `pip`, `npm`, and others. Instead, we typically containerize the application to make it self-contained along with all its dependencies so that it doesn't need to be installed. A container image is downloaded from a registry and run in a container engine such as Docker or Podman. There are also common techniques available to support multi-arch containers that will build and run on all the common micro-architectures listed previously, which is the approach we recommend using. See the following article for more information: `https://developers.redhat.com/articles/2021/08/26/introduction-nodejs-reference-architecture-part-5-building-good-containers`.

NOTE: Containers are not the only edge-native approach for isolating workloads. Enterprises may use **virtual machines** (**VMs**), serverless functions, or even WebAssembly (Wasm) depending on the code-base purpose, or execution environment. Regardless of the chosen approach, proper automation should be employed to ensure isolation is maintained.

Are the edge and the cloud extremes of the same thing?

In the previous paragraphs, we compared attributes of edge computing nodes largely by contrasting them with cloud computing hardware, connectivity, and facilities. Indeed, edge computing is largely distinguished from cloud computing by pointing out the differences and trade-offs, as depicted by the arrows at the bottom of the *LF Edge* diagram shown next:

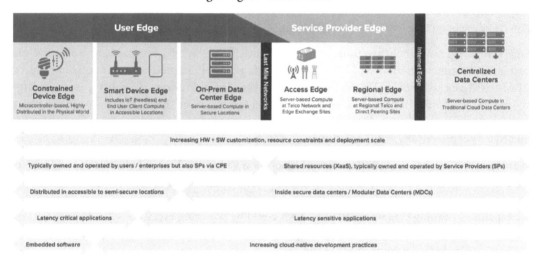

Figure 1.2 – The edge continuum with trade-offs shown at the bottom with gray arrows

Image Source: Linux Foundation Whitepaper

Jeff Ready, former CEO of Scale Computing, has a pithy way of contrasting the edge with the cloud:

"*The edge is really the inverse of the data center. A data center deployment is likely 1 or a small number of physical locations, hundreds of servers at those locations. The edge, on the other hand, is hundreds or thousands of locations, with often 1-3 servers at each one. You can't manage them the same way. You're still deploying thousands of servers, but with many, many locations you obviously can't have a team of IT pros at each one like you would in a datacenter. You need automated deployment, automated management, automated error recovery to make the edge work.*"

(https://blocksandfiles.com/2023/02/02/dell-vxrail-edge/)

Edge computing environments are very different from, and in most cases filling requirements that are the direct opposite of, cloud computing. As Eclipse's Mike Milinkovich has said: "*If you care about the physical location of your devices, then you are doing edge computing.*" However, edge computing has been established on a foundation of software development processes informed by cloud-native development best practices. In short, edge computing would not be possible if it weren't for the cloud.

How does edge computing bring value, and why now?

Edge computing reuses applicable cloud computing programming best practices, which give it a standard approach to software development that is fast, flexible, and works across multiple architectures. This methodology provides small teams with minimal cross-architecture experience in a way to create cross-platform distributed applications comprised of multiple loosely coupled services. This is what powers edge computing (and cheap computing).

Edge computing came about at a time when inexpensive but powerful compute became plentiful and custom fabrication tools more widely available. The Raspberry Pi single-board computer introduced ARM-based processors to hobbyists around the world at affordable prices while also spawning a large ecosystem of software utilities and hardware add-on boards. Since these systems could run many common Linux variants, they also formed the basis for **proofs of concept** (**POCs**) that could be easily turned into commercially viable solutions.

We're now beginning to see a similar wave of innovation with RISC-V-based systems that will further enable low-powered and efficient solutions that could even be embedded into standard hardware components. This would bring us to a point where computers with a Linux operating system that are capable of running containerized workloads could be powering every household appliance and consumer device or component. For example, Intensivate is running containers on the RISC-V ISA-compatible SoC that controls SSD drives.

By virtue of having inexpensive but powerful compute available and placed adjacent to where data is being generated, and being able to program that compute using existing tools and methods, you can simultaneously reduce the cost of computation while decreasing response times and reducing latency. Complex analytics no longer require offloading to the cloud, but ultimately, the available trade-offs largely depend on which edge you choose for workload placement.

Which edge? Categorizing edges

In this section, we cover the names and characteristics of various edge categories (or *edges*) that are commonly used, including which terms have been deprecated or have fallen out of the vernacular. By the end, you should be able to list the edges and describe the benefits and drawbacks of each, as shown in exhaustive detail next (*Figure 1.3*):

Attribute	User Edge			Last Mile Networks	Service Provider Edge		Centralized Cloud Data Centers
	Constrained Device Edge	Smart Device Edge	On-prem Data Center Edge		Access Edge	Regional Edge	
Hardware Class	Constrained microcontroller-based embedded devices (e.g. voice control speakers, thermostats, light switches, sensors, actuators, controllers). KBs to low MBs of available memory.	Arm and x86-based gateways, embedded PCs, hubs, routers, servers, small clusters. >256MB of available memory but still constrained. Accelerators (e.g. GPU, FPGA, TPU) depending on need.	Standard servers and networking with accelerators		Standard servers and networking with accelerators, telco radio infrastructure	Standard servers and networking with accelerators	Standard servers and networking with accelerators
Deployment Locations	Highly distributed in the physical world, embedded in discrete products and systems	Distributed in field, outside of secure data centers (e.g. factory floor, equipment closet, smart home) or embedded within distributed systems (e.g. connected vehicle, wind turbine, streetlight in public R.O.W.)	Secure, on-premise data-centers and micro-data centers (MDCs), e.g. located within an office building or factory. Typically owned and operated by enterprises.		CO, RO, Satellite DCs, owned and operated by service providers (e.g. ISPs, CSPs). Resources can also be located at User Edge in the case of CPE owned and managed by a service provider	CO, RO, Satellite DCs, owned and operated by service providers (e.g. ISPs, CSPs).	Centralized DCs, Zones, Regions owned and operated by CSPs. Compute in DCs located near key network
Global Node Footprint	Trillions	Billions	Millions		Hundreds of Thousands	Tens of Thousands	Hundreds
Role/ Function	Fixed to limited function applications, rely on higher-class-es of compute for advanced processing. Emerging simple ML capability via TinyML	Hyperlocal general compute for apps and services. Dynamic, SW-defined configuration with limited scalability. Includes IoT Compute Edge (headless systems) and End User devices	Local general compute for applications and services with moderate scalability. Dedicated to a specific enterprise.		Providing last mile access to the internet for users/enterprises. High availability, pubic and private, general and special. Broad scalability. Shared resources for IaaS, PaaS, SaaS, SDN (XaaS).	High availability, pubic and private, general and special. Broad scalability. Shared resources for IaaS, PaaS, SaaS, SDN (XaaS).	Hyperscale or webscale, public, general purpose. Public cloud involved shared resources for IaaS, PaaS, SaaS, SDN (XaaS).
Software Architecture	Embedded software/ firmware. Real-time Operating Systems (RTOS) for time-critical applications.	Bare metal to containerized/ virtualized depending on capability and use case. Linux, Windows and mobile OS'es (e.g. Android, iOS).	Virtualized, containerized and clustered compute. Linux and Windows.		Virtualized, containerized and clustered compute. VNF, CNF, managed services, networking. Linux and Windows.	Virtualized, containerized and clustered compute. VNF, CNF, managed services, networking. Linux and Windows.	Bare metal, VMs, Clusters, Containers, all architectures, all services. Linux and Windows.
Security, M&O	Specialized OTA M&O tools, often custom by device/manu-facturer. May rely on higher-class compute for security.	Require specific security and M&O tools due to resource constraints, unique functionality, accessibility and limited field technical expertise. Often unable to rely on a network firewall.	Evolution of cloud data center security and M&O tools to support distributed Kubernetes clusters. Benefits from physical and network security of purpose-built data centers.		Evolution of cloud data center security and M&O tools to support distributed Kubernetes clusters in regional locations	Evolution of cloud data center security and M&O tools to support distributed Kubernetes clusters in regional locations	Traditional cloud data-center security and M&O tools
Physical Attributes	Highly-specific form factors for every device	Diverse mix of specialized form-factors with unique I/O, industrial ruggedization, regulatory certifications, etc. based on use case	General purpose server-class infrastructure with some ruggedization and regulatory considerations (e.g. for MDCs)		Purpose-built radio infrastructure. General purpose server and networking hardware. Power, thermal, ruggediza-tion and regulatory considerations for localized resources.	General purpose server and networking infrastructure with power, thermal, ruggedization and regulatory considerations for localized resources	General purpose server infrastructure

Figure 1.3 – Detailed benefits and drawbacks of each edge

Image Source: Linux Foundation Whitepaper

The user edge – field-deployed compute

A fundamental confusion that commonly comes up in conversations revolves around *where* people think the edge is. One idea in people's minds is that "the edge" may be in houses, commercial offices, factories, vehicles, and utility shacks on the side of the road or at the base of a cell tower. These types of locations are typically thought of as the **far edge** because they are farthest away from a DC or cloud on a network and typically beyond the **last mile** of an SP network – hence, they are at the *edge* of a network or the farthest possible location on the network from a peering point or exchange.

But, the far edge is not the only location where edge computing takes place. The Linux Foundation's *LF Edge* organization refers to all edge computing locations falling after the last mile as belonging to the **user edge**, which follows a nomenclature categorizing types of computing by the *owner* of that compute. The fundamental assumption is that infrastructure at these locations is typically not shared beyond a single organization, business, or person. The Eclipse Foundation's *Edge Native Working Group* terms it **Field Deployed** while seeing the last mile and its associated infrastructure collectively as **Access-Transport**, as shown in *Figure 1.4*:

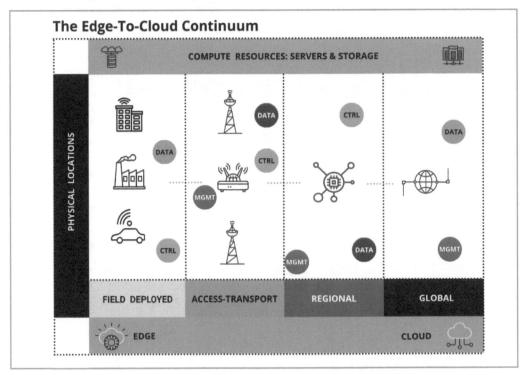

Figure 1.4 – Eclipse Foundation Edge Native Working Group terms for edge

Image Source: Eclipse Foundation Whitepaper

The SP edge – regional compute

On the other side of that last mile network connection, but beyond the edge of the internet's network infrastructure, is compute typically referred to as **telco infrastructure** belonging to **communication SPs** (**CSPs**). Satellite locations would be termed **central offices** (**COs**), and larger hubs would be **regional offices** (**ROs**). CSPs themselves are now comprised of phone companies (telcos and mobile operators or **mobile virtual network operators** (**MVNOs**)), **content distribution networks** (**CDNs**), and newer edge providers. They operate and offer programmable compute consisting of both software-enabled communications equipment and a limited amount of traditional racks of compute. *LF Edge* terms this collective category as the **SP edge**. The *Edge Native Working Group* calls this category simply **regional** and avoids associating it exclusively with SPs.

As the field of IoT computing was maturing, but before edge computing had gained widespread adoption, Cisco and others began using the term **fog computing** to refer to a method of distributing key cloud-like computing and storage infrastructure and services outside of the cloud and closer to devices. The term never entered widespread usage and was soon supplanted by the more general term **edge computing** to cover all computing outside of the cloud on programmable devices.

And lastly, you have traditional DCs. These are locations where physical access is controlled, racks of homogenous compute hardware are provided and remotely manageable, and both **Platform-as-a-Service** (**PaaS**) and **Infrastructure-as-a-Service** (**IaaS**) are offered. These DCs are typically owned and used by a single party, but mostly only differ from the cloud or global compute by size and scale. Large DCs such as these are rarely referred to as locations where edge computing happens; however, they are technically part of the edge as long as they reside outside of the internet's network.

Your computer or mine? Tactics for service deployment

In this section, we review different scenarios where more than one application or service can be deployed and running concurrently. We will give an example of each and discuss the purpose of that approach. By the end, you should recognize when each tactic is required.

Edge computing doesn't require dedicated resources

In *Sharpening the Edge*, the author refers to **edge computing** as primarily using your own systems, while **cloud computing** involves sharing systems and infrastructure with others. This simplification is largely correct at the macro scale, although edge computing can also involve sharing: by running multiple applications on a single device at the same time for multiple users, or sequentially at regularly scheduled intervals (day versus night, weekdays versus weekends, business open versus business closed). In the case of CSP-hosted edge infrastructure, it could even include hosting applications from multiple tenants each in an isolated environment on shared edge devices or clusters like cloud providers would. Let's take a deeper look at examples of each type of sharing in turn.

Single device, running multiple applications simultaneously

In a New England-based chip factory in late 2022, as reported by IBM in a blinded case study, IT staff deployed cameras containing a CPU and GPU capable of running Linux and containers. On those cameras, they placed containerized applications and ML models to detect if persons were wearing protective equipment, if the equipment was being worn properly, and if they maintained a safe distance from hazardous locations.

This involved multiple containers for object detection, object recognition, and object placement, as well as for sending messages and relevant screen captures extracted from video (with individual identities blurred out to preserve privacy) when infractions were detected above a specified level of certainty. The messages were sent over the local Wi-Fi network to an application on the shift manager's mobile phone *within seconds of detection* whereby the receiving application alerted the manager to investigate further if the provided still image appeared to warrant it.

Before edge computing devices made this possible, a solution would have been built to stream video to the cloud where inferencing would have been performed. By the time the manager would have been informed, minutes would have passed, and the individuals would likely no longer be in the area. Edge computing removed the expense of transporting video feeds to the cloud, reduced the resulting inferencing latency, eliminated any cloud computing costs, and ultimately ensured that the manager was notified up to 3 or more minutes sooner.

Before the cloud, the factory would have sent **closed-circuit television** (CCTV) feeds to a monitoring location where one or more persons would have viewed a bank of screens looking for issues on low-resolution displays, and called a manager if they spotted any issues. This approach would have been even more expensive and slow, and thus only likely to have been used to prevent major losses or accidents, or recorded and reviewed by investigators at a later time to determine potential causes of an accident.

Single device, alternating applications by schedule or purpose

In a grocery store, low-resolution video cameras stream feeds to constrained edge nodes attached to cameras containing low-power CPUs and limited RAM. These compute devices can run limited inferencing in a single container using tiny ML models at a few frames per second.

With those capabilities, they are used during store hours for spill detection or traffic counting when pointed at an aisle, dwell time when pointed at an end cap, and shelf restocking when pointed at a row. After the store is closed, those applications are replaced by a security application that looks for the presence of persons when the location should be unoccupied.

Edge computing makes these capabilities possible at an operating cost of pennies per day and without needing more connectivity than a local network connection.

Hosted edge infrastructure – applications on shared compute

An edge SP that began by providing only network peering with internet backbones and cloud providers has now begun offering bare-metal servers with connectivity to one or more providers of customer choice and large amounts of low-cost bandwidth. They do not provide infrastructure or platform services, making their offering ideal for customers who need always-on, reliable, inexpensive connectivity while at the same time providing low latencies due to physical proximity to customer facilities.

Hosted edge nodes are ideal for supplementing customer edge workloads temporarily while also avoiding the vendor lock-in of proprietary cloud solutions. The drawback to using hosted nodes is that the customer will need to provide any infrastructure and platform services and support. But it makes for an excellent extension or overflow to existing customer DCs or for situations when a company outgrows its existing locations but has not yet secured new facilities.

It also works well for temporary events, especially when they take place in a specific or limited geographical area. To that end, there is even a start-up that will deliver a self-contained edge DC in a container to your location for as long as you need it.

Cloud-out versus edge-in

Another common way of describing an architecture is based on its foundation and assumptions, and in what direction and manner it grows as its scope and responsibilities increase. If it starts out based in the cloud, using cloud-native best practices, and then later adds on capabilities that allow it to run in some fashion on the edge, that approach is described as **cloud-out**. On the other hand, if it starts out on the edge using edge-native development best practices, and then bursts to (hybrid) cloud infrastructure, that would be termed **edge-in**. Let's look at each in turn, go over an example, and discuss their relative strengths and weaknesses.

Looking deeper at cloud-out architectures

Cloud-out architectures begin with the cloud; that is, with global compute infrastructure using cloud-native development best practices. While *Chapter 11* will discuss these practices in depth, let's list an abbreviated version to frame the discussion:

- Package independent, autonomous services in lightweight containers or other abstractions
- Develop in the most appropriate language and/or framework for the purpose
- Compose with loosely coupled microservices
- Provide API-centric interfaces supporting common protocols and conventions
- Deliver a clean **separation of concerns** (**SoC**), especially between stateless and stateful services
- Abstract from underlying dependencies, both hardware and operating system
- Deploy on elastic infrastructure to automate scale-up and scale-out

- Rely on independent, automated application lifecycle management
- Implement **configuration as code (CaC)** maintained within an agile process
- Define resource allocation through declarative policies

Source: `https://thenewstack.io/cloud-native/10-key-attributes-of-cloud-native-applications/`

Looking at the preceding summary, a good example of the cloud-out approach to application development would be building a product using the SaaS model. SaaS is a way of building and delivering software so that it does not need to be installed (it is hosted by someone, usually in the cloud), and it does not need to be purchased (it is paid by subscription). Access can be provided in a browser or over the internet via APIs.

SaaS solutions demonstrate the cloud-out approach because they are typically hosted in the cloud, implemented with microservices, abstracted from dependencies, and deployed on elastic infrastructure. Individual SaaS offerings may also follow many other cloud-native best practices, but compliance with those principles is not obvious without access to the source code.

SaaS solutions clearly do not demonstrate the edge-in approach because they are not typically built to handle dependency unavailability (hence built with highly available architectural principles), service portability, target system constraints (since they do not need to be installed or remotely deployed), and dependence on orchestration. Additionally, they presume an always-on network connection with low latency and high throughput.

So the pros of the SaaS architecture approach are that the application and its constituent services do not need to be built for wide micro-architecture compatibility and thus can be narrowly tailored to the deployment target's specific hardware requirements. It can rely on the hosting facility provider to maintain and support the infrastructure, platform, and connectivity as well as the facilities themselves. And within reason, they can scale horizontally up to the provider's available capacity.

The cons of this approach are that the application and services may be narrowly tailored to the environment and are thus not inherently portable, and the risk of vendor lock-in is considerable. This may also render the application brittle when exposed to new or unanticipated conditions, thus requiring more ongoing maintenance than if it had been built using edge-native principles. Finally, a SaaS service will clearly be unavailable in the absence of a network connection.

Delving into edge-in architectures

Edge-in architectures start with field-deployed compute and adhere to the edge-native programming model. *Chapter 11* will cover this topic in greater detail, so here's a quick summary:

- Tolerate interruptions and unavailability of service dependencies and connectivity
- Design for service operational portability between system tiers

- Avoid explicit dependence on container orchestration features

- Employ external application configuration and secrets per instance, including support for runtime updates

- Anticipate system-imposed constraints

- Ensure services are self-contained

- Follow data privacy regimes based on target requirements

- Leverage platform-provided services when possible

Source: `https://www.ibm.com/docs/en/eam/4.5?topic=clusters-edge-native-development-best-practices`

Based on the preceding points, a good example of an application following this approach would be one or more multi-arch containerized gardening applications running on a Raspberry Pi, which is connected to moisture, light, humidity, and temperature sensors. The application can retrieve data from the sensors, persist it locally, and make it available through a web application displaying a page with the data or making it available through a REST API as a data payload.

This architecture follows edge-in principles due to its ability to collect data from a sensor while it is connected, to provide the collected data while it maintains a network connection, and to resume operation when rebooted or after an interruption of power. The applications are portable and can be run on multiple architectures, providing that sensors are present on that machine. They do not require the orchestration that Kubernetes provides. They do not require services residing on another machine; the data stays resident on the machine itself unless manually moved.

The application architecture does not demonstrate a cloud-out approach because it may not be abstracted from the underlying hardware dependencies (the sensors), and it does not use elastic infrastructure to scale.

So, the benefits of this approach are that the solution is resilient to adverse conditions and can function fine without an internet or network condition, being completely self-contained. It also runs on inexpensive hardware and would cost pennies in electricity to operate monthly. And when the hardware eventually fails, it is cheap to replace.

Wrapping up, you've seen the differences between cloud-out and edge-in architectural principles, compared how they work in the real world and read about the pros and cons. Now, let's discuss the larger patterns that most applications follow on the edge … the archetypes.

Introducing archetype patterns

In this section, we introduce you to the concept of archetypes. Along the way, we cover the *days* involved in the software life cycle and discuss deployment methods. By the end, you will be ready to learn about and use archetype patterns.

What is an archetype?

An archetype is the original model or form of something that embodies all primary qualities of that item, whether that item is an abstract concept or a physical object. In the case of architectural patterns, our assertion is that most application architectures can be derived from an original pattern archetype (source) or a slight variation based on local or business considerations. Therefore, in this book, we attempt to tease out archetypes and discuss them at length based on our belief that identifying and mastering them will give you the foundational skills needed to tackle most, if not all, edge application scenarios. By following these patterns judiciously, you will be able to create solutions that are not only portable but also future-proof.

In the archetype-pattern diagrams to be found in this book, we will follow certain conventions:

- Show all elements of equal size and shape so as to imply that all components are of equal importance

- Refer to a component by its function or role instead of a product name, which emphasizes replaceability and a vendor-neutral approach

- Indicate placement by edge category as denoted in columns ranging from the cloud on the right to the field-deployed far edge on the left

- Draw rectangles around edge nodes to indicate placement of components, applications, and services

- Connect edge devices, nodes, systems, platforms, and infrastructure with arrows indicating the direction of data flow

See an example diagram at `https://wiki.edgexfoundry.org/display/FA/Open+Retail+Reference+Architecture?preview=/55705782/81625502/Open%20Retail%20Reference%20Architecture%20Diagram.png`.

Once you settle on an architecture pattern on day 0, based on the best fit to the requirements and business needs, the next consideration you need to address is how to deploy that architecture ... both on day 1 and maintaining it on days 2-N. Let's delve into the idea of days 0-N, which will also be used in *Chapter 7* when we discuss applying automation to these deployments.

The days of software creation

When you are involved in creating and launching a software product or an application, it is helpful to think about distinct blocks of work that are typically worked on at the same time. This categorization applies whether you work in project management, software architecture, or operations (DevOps or SRE). Those blocks or categories are denoted as "days" followed by a number to indicate where they fit in the sequence of events:

- Day 0 is when initial planning and preparation happen. These types of tasks involve designing, which can include traditional UX design, as well as application and information architecture.

The final product requirements should be specified, agreed to, and documented by the end of this timeframe. The goal of these tasks is to prepare for software development work to begin.

- Day 1 denotes programming, provisioning, and configuration of environments and pipelines. That would also include dependency installation, finalizing automation, and all unit and **end-to-end (E2E)** testing. At the end of this period, the application should be documented, approved by all relevant parties, and ready for launch into a production environment.

- Day 2 marks the support period where time is spent working on issues, optimization, A/B testing of new features, blue/green testing of differing versions, and so on. This time should also be used to build up a support database, any FAQs, and possibly training support chatbots or other automated response mechanisms.

- Day N (end) would then be for activities related to the retirement of an application and its provisioned environment, assets, and supporting infrastructure. By the end of this period, all traces of the application should be removed except for any items of historical value or required to be kept intact for legal retention purposes:

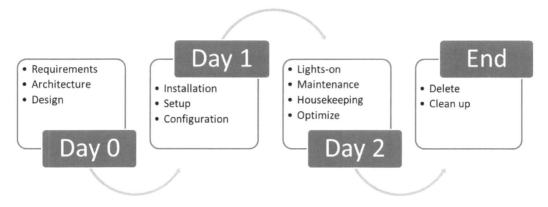

Figure 1.5 – Depiction of days 0-N categories with major activities shown in each

Image Source:: https://dzone.com/articles/defining-day-2-operations

Deploying archetype patterns

When it comes to deploying solutions that live entirely in the cloud, you can rely on IaaS and provider-specific deployment tools and configurations. This is made easier due to being able to integrate with **identity and access management (IAM)** solutions and because both managed and DIY components can be well integrated. Even when your solutions span multiple clouds, there are well-known open source deployment tools designed to abstract away cloud provider-specific details and allow you to focus on your specific tasks.

But when it comes to field-deployed solutions at the far edge, potential connectivity issues and heterogeneous systems, combined with a lack of infrastructure services, will require a different approach. We'll go into greater detail in *Chapters 9* and *11*, but using deployment and application life-cycle management tools that can operate autonomously and pulling configuration from a central control plane rather than pushing to the edge tend to resolve most of those deployment issues, including scalability and security.

Summary

In this chapter, you learned about what capabilities the edge and the cloud have in common, and what distinguishes one from the other when it comes to the tiers of compute: infrastructure, platforms, services, and applications.

We covered the names and characteristics of edge categories and described the benefits and drawbacks of each. We also discussed various ways that edge nodes can be shared between tasks. We described how an architecture can be scaled based on its scope and responsibilities with cloud-out and edge-in paradigms. Also, we introduced you to the concept of archetypes and the "days" involved in the software development life cycle.

Now, you should be ready to learn about the basic components and building blocks that go into archetype patterns. Just as importantly, we'll also discuss how to approach solutions from the right perspective in order to build a future-proof application, follow best practices, and use long-term thinking.

2

Edge Architectural Components

Edge computing architectures, although relatively new, have their origins in IoT architectures. There are a lot more devices in play now, some with compute and storage. These devices are key to edge computing architectures. The different sizes, form factors, the compute, and storage capacity of these edge devices make for many variations in solution architectures.

These solution architectures are unique because there are limitations at each layer, from device to compute to storage. Architects designing them often must think about the limitations, especially when it comes to the far-edge aspect. One must keep in mind the intrinsic benefits of edge computing such as low latency, high performance, less power consumption, high bandwidth, and multiple dispersed locations. Edge computing has given rise to a new paradigm of application architecture specifically designed to run in the distributed edge domain, which we call **edge-native applications**.

This chapter describes the four major roles of the components in an edge architecture. We then talk about the common functional and **non-functional requirements** (**NFRs**) and discuss the software and hardware components that commonly go into the creation of edge architectures. It concludes with a discussion of device architectures, data transmission protocols, and architectural decisions. The main topics are as follows:

- Edge components
- Functional requirements
- **Non-functional requirements** (**NFRs**)
- Use cases and patterns
- Architectural decisions

Edge components

There are four major roles for the edge components in an enterprise's edge computing architecture: edge devices, the edge gateway, or server in the enterprise edge (part of the user edge's field deployed compute), the micro data center in the Service Provider Edge's Regional Compute, and the enterprise cloud. The edge server not only acts as a gateway to connect all edge devices in a secure manner but also allows for the management of all those devices. See *Figure 2.1*:

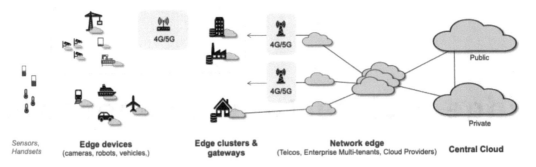

Figure 2.1 – Common representation of the edges in edge computing

The enterprise cloud is shown on the far right. This could be a public, private, or hybrid cloud, which is the domain of hyperscalers. To the left of it is the realm of regional compute, where the telcos or **communications service providers (CSPs)** operate. Next to it is the user edge (in this case, the *user* could be an enterprise) where the edge clusters and gateways are deployed. On the far left, IoT and edge devices are shown, including sensors, gauges, cameras, robots, and the like.

At a macro level, there are four aspects to an edge computing solution and you will see them reflected in the architecture diagrams that follow in this chapter. They are as follows:

- **Edge devices**: While some IoT devices such as sensors, gauges, and actuators cannot run any software, many edge devices have some computing power and some storage. That lets them store some data and run some simple analytics. Depending on their form factor, certain edge devices have enough compute, memory ranging from 128 MB to 256 MB, and almost 1 GB of storage, which is enough to analyze the data and perform real-time inferencing without needing to send the data to a backend server or the cloud. That is what edge-native computing is all about. If they are not using ARM architecture, the devices could be x86 class CPUs equipped with one or two cores.

  Note that now it is possible to deploy commodity AI accelerators connected to a USB port to supplement their inferencing and analytics capabilities.

- **Edge servers**: The other components in the user edge space are edge servers or **edge nodes**. There is a one-to-many relationship between an edge server and edge devices. Edge servers or gateways are constantly in touch with edge devices by way of agents running on the devices and are used to deploy applications onto those devices. These are typically **commercial off-the-shelf (COTS)** computers that could be located in a distributed facility such as a factory floor, store backroom, warehouse, or remote office. These could be ruggedized or placed in a protective enclosure. The small-sized machines have 8 cores, the medium-sized machines have 16 cores, and anything with more compute capacity would constitute a large machine. The memory in these machines starts at 16 GB RAM and they could have hundreds of gigabytes of storage. If inferencing at the device is insufficient, then data from the far-edge devices is sent to the edge server or even to the cloud for further analysis and deeper insights.

- **Regional compute or service provider edge**: This edge is sometimes also referred to as the network edge or micro data center. CSPs are taking advantage of newer networking technologies to create these *regional clouds* or *local clouds* that provide software-based infrastructure services for devices to communicate with at the far edge of the network. The major selling point of the telcos is that data from the edge devices does not have to be sent to the cloud but can reside in this *regional cloud*, thereby reducing the distance and time that data must travel. For the end user, it means decreased latency, better bandwidth, and more security. This is especially true with the use of 5G.

- **Enterprise cloud**: This is the centralized cloud that could be a public or private cloud or an on-premises data center. As is common to clouds, enterprises get unlimited compute and storage along with management capabilities, plus access to a growing portfolio of other cloud services. From an edge computing perspective, this is home to four facets: storage of most of the device data, device management at a global level, AI model building and training, and enterprise-level analytics.

Now that we have seen the major components that one finds in edge computing solutions, the next thing is to dive into some of the functional requirements that enterprises ask for.

Functional requirements

In *Chapter 1*, we talked about cloud-out and edge-in paradigms. Cloud-out is where computing is taken out of the data center and brought to the far edges of the network. Conversely, the movement of the generated data from the source or the edge to a location with more computational resources for analysis is the edge-in part. Those facets drive functional requirements in an edge computing solution. We will discuss the common functional requirements of an edge computing solution in the subsequent sections.

Sensing

This is where we still deal with traditional sensors (e.g., IoT/accelerometers, thermometers, or actuators) as architectural components that acquire data and help create a signal. When combining technologies such as edge and **artificial intelligence** (**AI**), you introduce new ways of designing and deploying technology, thus improving and automating situational awareness with sense-making systems. These are deployed in stores, shop floors, industrial equipment, mines, and even in vehicles.

They are often referred to as systems that have situational awareness. These sense-making systems fuse human-like thinking with sensing technologies so they can take actionable insights to augment humans in their work or help humans. Additionally, such systems can support **augmented reality** (**AR**) deployments by providing data that will be "visible" to humans working nearby. That is the core idea of these edge computing patterns. Businesses that want to create edge/IoT solutions should have a good understanding of their assets, especially their people, because that helps them in making better decisions while incorporating this newly enabled sensing technology.

Inferencing

Inferencing, by definition, is the act of reasoning from factual knowledge. Inferencing at the edge means providing actionable intelligence using AI-powered techniques based on the data gathered by different types of devices, such as sensors, cameras, microphones, and so on. One of the outcomes of real-time inferencing at the source of the data is a better security posture. This is because data does not have to travel too far, which reduces the attack area.

Analytics

Edge analytics is the ability of **machine learning** (**ML**) models deployed on edge devices outside of the cloud or data center so that deeper analysis of the collected data can be done. The creation, training, and retraining of models are typically done on the user edge or the service provider edge.

Depending on the industry scenario involving imagery, the requirement aspects can expand to include image classification, object detection, and anomaly detection. While visual edge analytics is most obvious and common, we should point out that there are many other types of data produced by IoT-type devices that get analyzed – temperature sensors on freezers and ovens, shock and vibration analyzers on wheels and other moving parts, noise detectors to isolate certain types of noise, flow meters for liquids, pressure gauges in industrial settings, and speech and tone analysis. Collision avoidance systems in many new automobiles use multiple proximity sensors in lieu of cameras, while others use LiDAR technology.

The lifeblood of the three functional requirements mentioned so far is data. So, it behooves us to talk about data as one of the key requirements. *Chapter 6* does take an in-depth view of data.

> Reminders
>
> **LiDAR** stands for **light detection and ranging**. It is a technology that uses laser light to measure the distance between objects. It is used in autonomous vehicles, astronomy, and other applications.

Data

Whether it is audio, visual, telemetry, or sensor data, it is all about the generation, collection, movement, and analysis of data in an edge computing solution. Ensuring the data doesn't have to travel far allows it to be analyzed more quickly. And, in case the data must be sent to an edge server, it takes less time compared to a traditional centralized cloud environment.

In any IT solution architecture, more so in edge computing architecture, the questions that solution architects are faced with are the following:

- Where should the data be sent to be stored?
- Where should the data be sent to be analyzed?

The solution architect must also determine whether it is critical to analyze the data at the source in real time and whether the data calls for more in-depth analysis in the future. Whether or not to store the data generated by the devices depends largely on business and jurisdictional compliance requirements.

Another view is to take a t-shirt-sized approach. Remember the footprint of the deployed applications ranges from being large to medium to small as you move away from the cloud – that is, going from right to left in *Figure 2.1*. While real-time inferencing is done by the far-edge devices, some of the deeper rules-based or even neural network-based analytics take place in the middle layers, while ML model building, training, and retraining, which require a lot more computing power, end up being performed in the layers to the right.

> **Reminders**
>
> **Inference** is coming to a conclusion based on evidence and reasoning.
>
> **Analysis** is the process of methodically breaking something down to gain a better understanding of it.

Some of the common functional requirements have been discussed. There could be more, depending on the industrial use cases.

In the next section, we look at the non-functional requirements.

Non-functional requirements

Edge computing architectures must satisfy several NFRs. While low latency and high bandwidth are two of the most common and obvious requirements, enterprises often list security as their most important requirement. The other NFRs are related to service management and operations.

Security

When discussing inferencing, we mentioned that one of the outcomes of real-time inferencing at the source of the data is a better security posture since data doesn't have to travel far, thus reducing the attack area. That said, any and all data in transit must be sent using a secure protocol. Onboarded devices could use keys, security certificates, or both. As in all IT solutions, components in an edge solution more often than not must meet regulatory, compliance, and local security standards because they deal with data. For a discussion of this topic in depth, see *Chapter 6*, where we cover security aspects of data in motion and data at rest.

Service management and operations

Given that an edge computing solution can have many edge devices and that these devices could be installed in remote or hard-to-reach locations, there are specific NFRs related to service management and operations that are described here:

- **Availability**: Availability is key in an edge computing architecture. The edge devices must always be available to gather or create data, and the solution must continue to operate even when there is no connectivity – that is, in a disconnected mode. It is important to eliminate all **single points of failure** (**SPOFs**) from the solution.

- **Reliability**: This is the other side of the availability coin. In certain edge devices such as moving vehicles, safety-related computations must always return correct results in a predictable timeframe, even if this decreases the overall availability of the system. A device can be available but may or may not be reliable, whereas a reliable device will have high availability.

- **Latency**: Because edge computing is so tightly tied to the network, you commonly hear about latency and bandwidth. Getting data from the devices and acting upon that data expeditiously is critical. Reduced latency is one of the primary requirements in any edge solution.

- **Resiliency**: The ability of a system to manage itself is important. This requirement refers to internal failures as opposed to external ones. When conditions change, are the agreements between the devices and the edge hub immediately terminated or refreshed? Make sure that agents and services are always in a well-defined state.

- **Scalability**: Scalability, when it comes to the number of devices deployed and the management of those devices, is usually an assumed requirement, and this can range from tens to thousands to millions of devices. Systems must be designed to handle the onboarding and deployment of any number of edge devices and edge servers. *Figure 2.2* shows the scaling going from right to left:

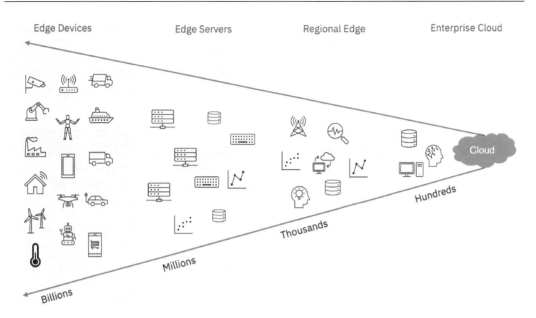

Figure 2.2 – Edge computing at scale

- **Maintainability**: Given that there might be thousands of devices, often in remote locations, maintaining them on a regular basis becomes an important requirement. Having a planned maintenance schedule with specific maintenance scenarios addresses this requirement. But what about unplanned maintenance? One might argue that unplanned maintenance is exactly what edge solutions are designed to prevent and handle.

We've talked about requirements, both functional and non-functional. Remember, there may be more, depending on the use case. Let's look at some of the common edge use cases.

Edge use cases and patterns

Edge use cases depend a lot on the industry that is targeted. So do the related applications that get deployed on the devices that generate or collect data. While the software stack might be similar, the form factor of the devices in play will determine the size and complexity of the applications. The applications will depend on the use cases relevant to a particular industry. For example, a camera might be trained differently when acting as a security camera than one looking for welding defects on a manufacturing shop floor. The devices are similar, in that they are both cameras, but the application or workload running on them is different depending on their function.

Edge workloads are often used to describe any edge-hosted service. Any software application that has utility when running in an edge node can be described as an edge workload. Such functionality is usually delivered as microservices running in Docker containers or related container technology, but it can have other forms as well. Examples of edge services include vibration analysis, visual recognition, acoustic insights, speech recognition, and so on. Solution architects must decide on what workloads run where based on device constraints and also the data posture.

While not exhaustive, *Table 2.1* captures some of the common edge use cases (see `https://www.redhat.com/en/blog/edge-automation-seven-industry-use-cases-and-examples` for reference):

Category	Brief description
Manufacturing operations	Automation of factory operations and quality improvement analysis, enabled by data collection from sensors, connected metrology systems, and AI. Includes root cause analysis for identification and correction of process issues.
Manufacturing quality inspection	Using visual data Visual inspection for manufacturing plants, industrial equipment products, and transportation. Helps identify potential issues in the use and production of equipment through visual inspection of products.
	Using acoustic data Manufacturing quality inspection (AI acoustics) on the plant process floor using acoustic data for quality – for example, sounds of welds during robotic processes or sounds of motors in engine rooms indicating damage.
Asset management/ supply chain	Remote tracking, monitoring, and predictive maintenance of heavy equipment and operator network equipment, and automation of field service maintenance. Also includes remote monitoring and tracking of moveable items such as freight, food, and animals.
Public safety and emergency response	Connected systems to monitor, alert, and coordinate responses to public safety incidents and environmental issues. Includes in-car camera systems and body-worn cameras used by public safety officials.
Transportation infrastructure management	Use of sensors to enable real-time monitoring, adjustment, and maintenance of transport infrastructure, road traffic, and airport facilities. Includes the automation of public transportation systems.
Predictive maintenance and asset reliability	Using high-volume sensors, IoT, weather, and fleet data to predict reliability or optimize assets based on resource health insights from operational data and analytics. Leverages device telemetry to create a digital twin model of physical equipment.

Connected vehicles*	Connected vehicles that enable coordination with infrastructure (V2I) and other cars (V2V), deliver content through infotainment systems, and feed data to insurers. Also includes fleet management for coordination of fleets of vehicles and tracking of vehicles for security.
Smart retail	Use of real-time sensors, displays, and connectivity in and around retail stores. Enables personalized digital signage, context-sensitive in-store marketing, insights into buying behaviors at the point of sale, and monitoring and adjustment of inventories.
Smart home	Connected home systems to monitor and manage security, such as perimeter breaches, as well as other home functions such as energy usage, lighting, heating, and locks. Does not include smart utility meters, home entertainment, media devices, or gaming consoles.
Financial crime prevention	Leverage applications for preventing fraud and security lapses; Edge provides the ability to run crime checks across different regulatory boundaries – for example, international banks.
Secure healthcare systems	By deploying secure edge apps across clinic and hospital locations, medical records and other sensitive patient data are encrypted when transmitted or stored and is often anonymized when accessed by other systems and non-essential personnel.
Building automation	By leveraging actuators, sensors, and control systems in buildings to monitor and control various aspects such as HVAC, energy, lighting, and security, edge computing enhances building automation systems. While the term "smart home" covers things inside the home, **building automation system (BAS)** deals with the services around and about the building.

Table 2.1 – Edge use cases

`* Software Defined Vehicle (SDV) builds on the connected car concept. It is a vehicle in which all the features and functions are controlled and driven by software. Whether it is the vehicle controls or infotainment system, the driver and passengers interact directly with the in-vehicle software platform` (https://www.ibm.com/blog/the-software-defined-vehicle-the-architecture-behind-the-next-evolution-of-the-automotive-industry/).

The use cases are dependent on the industry and the edge devices depend on those industry use cases. In the following section, we list some of the device specifications and the data transmission protocols used by the devices.

Edge device specifications and protocols

Chapter 1 talked about the typical chip configurations used in edge computing solutions. They are listed again here for completeness:

- x86_64 or AMD64

- ARM32 or ARM6, ARM7

- ARM64 or armhf, including Apple M1 and M2

- ppc64le

- RISC-V

- S390x (typically running LinuxONE)

Edge device types include gauges, sensors, actuators, cameras, robots, and other IoT core devices. These days, drones and automobiles have become the ultimate device types at the edge.

Some of these devices do not have any compute or storage capacity. In those cases, the devices gather or generate data that is transmitted to the nearest edge server or gateway acting as a hub (some refer to this sector as the first mile). That data, depending on its type, can be sent using any of the different protocols that are available. *Table 2.2* lists some of the common data transfer protocols we see. The protocols are listed in alphabetical order and do not distinguish between wired and software protocols. We have also included some of the legacy protocols such as BACnet and Modbus:

Protocol	Description
BACnet	BACnet is a communications protocol designed to allow communication of building automation and control systems.
Bluetooth LE	Bluetooth Low Energy is a wireless personal area network technology used by many modern-day devices.
HTTP/HTTPS	Hypertext Transfer Protocol/Secure are communications protocols that are stateless. They are the foundation of the internet.
Kafka	Apache Kafka is an event streaming platform used to collect, process, store, and integrate data at scale.
LoRa	LoRa (Long Range) is a physical proprietary radio communication technique.
Modbus	Modbus is a data communications protocol for use with programmable logic controllers.
MQTT	Originally an initialism for MQ Telemetry Transport, this is a lightweight publish/subscribe machine-to-machine messaging connectivity protocol. Now there is Sparkplug from Eclipse Foundation that provides MQTT protocol, ideal for industrial automation.

ONVIF	ONVIF is a standard for how IP products within video surveillance and other physical security areas can communicate with each other.
OPC UA	OPC Unified Architecture is a cross-platform, open source standard for data exchange from sensors to cloud applications.
RTSP	Real-Time Streaming Protocol is a stateful protocol used for video contribution.
Streams over HTTP	One of many HTTP-based adaptive protocols.
WebRTC	WebRTC is a combination of standards, protocols, and JavaScript and HTML5 APIs that enables real-time communications.
Z-Wave	Z-Wave is a wireless communications protocol used primarily for residential and commercial building automation.
ZigBee	ZigBee is a wireless technology that uses the packet-based radio protocol intended for low-cost, battery-operated devices in industrial settings.

Table 2.2 – Data transmission protocols

The block architecture diagram shown in *Figure 2.3* depicts the data flow between various edge-related components. Representative latency times between the different layers are shown in milliseconds at the top:

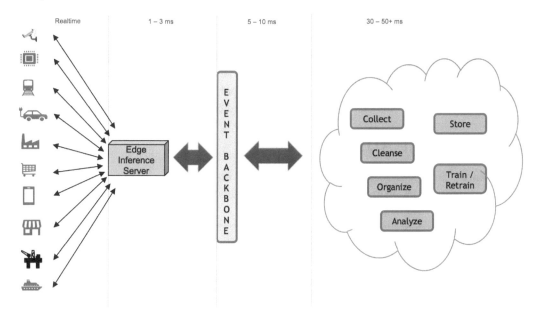

Figure 2.3 – A representative data flow in edge computing

The software stack in an edge solution architecture, as mentioned earlier, will vary depending on the use case, and edge use cases vary based on industry scenarios. No matter the industry, an edge computing topology involves a combination of hardware devices and software products. At the far edge, if possible, devices would run a containerized inference model in edge-native mode. These could be vision models, audio classification models, or sensory processing models. If not, the data would be sent to an inference edge server. Non-visual data, such as telemetry data and events, is typically sent to the communication layer known as the event backbone, which then would be routed to the appropriate destination. Software capable of training or retraining AI/ML models, including messaging, data, and AI-related middleware, could be aggregated, cleansed, and analyzed or stored in the next layer with more compute and storage.

As noted in *Chapter 1*, containers are not the only edge-native approach for isolating workloads, including inference models. Enterprises may use **virtual machines** (**VMs**), serverless functions, or even **web assembly** (**Wasm**), depending on the code base purpose or execution environment. Regardless of the chosen approach, proper automation should be employed to ensure isolation is maintained.

Architectural decisions

Solution architects are familiar with **architectural decisions** (**ADs**) when designing IT architectures. They are meant to capture key design issues and provide the rationale for selecting one of many alternatives in a solution. These decisions concern the design of a software system as a whole or one or more of its core components or connectors. They are made after considering various alternatives within a given aspect or domain.

Similarly, there are many facets that solution architects must decide on when designing edge solutions. It could be choosing the most appropriate transfer protocol to get data from a particular device, the type and location of storage, the use of private 5G versus public 5G, or the size and model of the edge server/cluster. These and other aspects must be considered before settling on a solution architecture.

Grouping edge ADs

Components in an edge architecture are broadly grouped into four domains that map to deployment areas. This is where solution architects have to make architectural design decisions. *Figure 2.4* shows the four component domains:

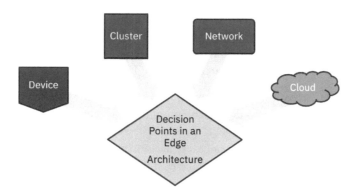

Figure 2.4 – The four decision points affecting edge architecture

Each of these domains has its own nuances and is equally important. And there are sub-domains within them, as shown in *Table 2.3*:

Component area	Description and sub-domains
Cloud and data	Cloud deployment model. The nature of the business and compliance requirements will dictate whether to use a private, public, hybrid, or distributed cloud. Additionally, data storage decisions will also determine data store type and size.
Network	The most important component. In choosing the most optimal network design, architects have to weigh cost and availability and the nature of the business. There is 4G, Wi-Fi, 5G public, or 5G private. Now there are even different types of **RAN** (**radio access network**) to choose from. That said, at times there won't be any network connectivity, so one has to plan for disconnected operations, which is covered in later chapters.
Edge server/cluster	Role and location of edge server or cluster. This determines not only the size but also the number of edge clusters/servers to deploy in order to support various devices.
Edge device	Device type and form factor. This determines the type of applications that can be deployed on a given device and the data transfer protocol to use.

Table 2.3 – Edge computing components

Solution architects should pay special attention to networking because of the recent advances in network technology, especially with the advent of 5G, which introduced, among other features, **software-defined networking** (**SDN**). While it is not explicitly called out, there is a cost dimension to all these ADs that could affect the final architecture.

As mentioned earlier, each of these four domains has sub-domains and decision points that can overwhelm solution architects who design end-to-end edge solutions. The crux of any AD is to justify the choice of a particular component. We have listed some of the more common ADs in the following section with the knowledge that not every decision point would be relevant to every solution architecture. Again, we go from right to left – that is, from the cloud to the devices.

Cloud

The standard cloud deployment models are well-known – public cloud, private cloud, and hybrid cloud. We would be remiss to not mention the new distributed deployment model, which is described in *Chapter 5*. The cloud deployment model choice depends on the industry for which the edge solution is designed. As an example, the banking industry has stringent requirements on where data can be stored and even how it is stored. With such requirements in mind, the only option then is to use a private cloud.

AD #	Requirement	Factors affecting decision
C001	Cloud deployment model	A private, public, or hybrid cloud model decision must be made based on bandwidth, latency, and cost. Always consider the optimal use between a physical data center, an on-premises cloud, a public cloud, or an acceptable combination.
	Data storage	No matter which cloud model is chosen, the next decision point in edge computing is about data. Architects must consider where to store different types of data. Enterprises might agree to store generic data in the cloud, but business-sensitive data may need to be stored on-premises and be encrypted. The other key aspect is data sovereignty, which is covered in *Chapter 6*. Sometimes, it is mandated by regulations, and in other cases, it is desirable because of the social or political environment.

C002	Cloud resource usage	The cloud offers unlimited resources when it comes to compute, data, and storage. Hence, it is more suited to build, train, and retrain ML models in the cloud rather than at the edge.
	Data storage	Since there is so much data generated, the question of the use and storage of data and other cloud resources must be considered. It affects the deployment of ML applications and also the training or retraining of the ML models.

Table 2.4 – Cloud-related ADs

Network

Enterprises have the choice between private networks that are highly secure, single-tenant networks, and multi-tenant carrier networks offered by telcos. With 5G technology, we have seen a rise in private wireless networks. In choosing the type of network, solution architects must take into account the use case requirements, location, and cost. To add to the complexity, there are two types of networks – overlay and underlay.

The overlay network is a virtual network that operates on top of a physical infrastructure, the underlay. This abstraction model has opened new avenues of efficient network traffic routing. These new avenues affect both north-south and east-west traffic flows.

> **Reminder**
> North-south network traffic is the data flow to and from the cloud or data center. East-west network traffic is the data flow between deployed applications, amongst the components of applications, and to other cloud services.

Figure 2.5 shows, at a very high level, network traffic flow patterns. Prior to virtualization becoming mainstream, most network traffic would be in the north-south direction. As more applications moved to the cloud, combined with the proliferation of edge data centers and edge locations, the amount of east-west network traffic within the facility and intra-facility has outpaced north-south network traffic:

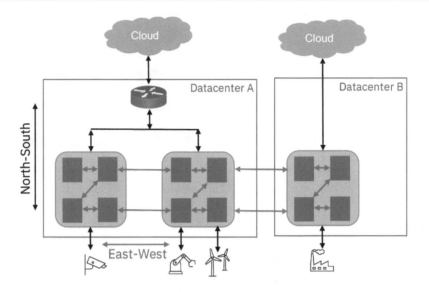

Figure 2.5 – Network traffic flow

Solution and network architects must pay close attention to southbound access interfaces of the edge computing domain because they impact the network access points and also affect the topology of the edge computing platform. Because data flow is multi-dimensional, two aspects should be considered when designing the southbound traffic management: security and futurizing the sensor network.

AD #	Requirement	Factors affecting decision
N001	Access termination technology	Coverage area, terrain, device age, and support for legacy interfaces affect this requirement.
		Whether it is tens of meters or many miles, the size of coverage area will determine whether to use 4G or 5G, a public or a private network, or even Wi-Fi.
		The terrain or facility construction also affects the choices. If the distance is less than 50 meters and the 4G or 5G spectrum is not available for some reason, then Wi-Fi might be the only access protocol option.
		While accounting for constrained computing form factor, low power, disconnected operations, and other networking challenges, architects must be aware that many legacy devices do not support the new cellular protocols. Wi-Fi is more prevalent, and sometimes, even that is not widely deployed. This leads to a closer look at gateway devices.

N002	Edge gateway protocol	Establishing a unified stream of highly heterogeneous interfaces supporting the edge devices/sensors is critical in edge computing architectures. REST, AMQP, XMPP, MQTT, and CoAP are some very device-specific protocols out there. Which one would be most efficient in a particular scenario is something solution architects must decide.
	Data transformation	Different data types generated at the edge call for different protocols and aggregation requiring data to be transformed before it can be consumed by the edge computing platform. Again, something the solution architect must decide is whether and where that should be done.
N003	Edge network domain	To design an edge solution that is efficient and cost-effective requires the application domain to adopt two things – an API-based control plane, **software-defined network** (**SDN**) or a "flat" overlay network. Additionally, this large-scale distributed application architecture must be secured while operating on constrained resources.

Edge solutions can use many microservices for different functions, from visual analytics to heat sensing. An overlay network could be used for communication between these microservices.

Which deployment domain is best suited is a question that architects must answer – Kubernetes, **function-as-a-service** (**FaaS**), or maybe even serverless? |

Table 2.5 – Network-related ADs

Server/cluster

As noted throughout the book, not all edge devices are created equal, especially when it comes to compute and storage. When IoT-type devices such as sensors, gauges, and actuators that do not have any compute or storage are part of an edge computing solution, an edge server or edge cluster is inserted and takes on the role of aggregating the data. In some cases, it is not viable to run a large ML application on the edge device, in which case that application would have to be deployed on the nearest edge server/cluster.

AD #	Requirement	Factors affecting decision
S001	Deployment of edge servers/clusters	The use case will determine whether an edge server/cluster is required, and if so, based on the application to be hosted and the data generated, the server specification will be determined. For example, in a retail scenario, cameras, inventory scanners, point-of-sale (POS) systems, and so on deployed in a large department store would have to be managed and monitored. Depending on customer traffic, sales volume, and store inventory, the solution architect would have to decide on the number and size of edge servers to configure.
S002	Edge hub location	Deciding where to place the edge hub – on-premises or in the cloud – is another key decision point. Again, it might depend on the industry use case. Typically, one edge hub is enough, but depending on the deployment topology, multiple edge hubs may be needed. For example, in healthcare and banking, industry regulations and/or government data sovereignty requirements will influence the edge hub location decision.

Table 2.6 – Compute-related ADs

Device

We have alluded to the fact that there are many different types of edge devices – audio devices, indoor and outdoor video cameras, light and motion sensors, heat sensors, vibration monitors, pressure gauges, and other telemetry devices. An edge solution topology could have a few of these edge devices or hundreds of them. In *Table 2.7*, we only focus on edge devices that are equipped with some computing power and storage capacity. From a data perspective, edge solutions should support one or more of the most common data transfer protocols that were listed in *Table 2.2*.

AD #	Requirement	Factors affecting decision
D001	Edge device registration	To be part of an edge solution, all edge devices that have some amount of compute and storage capacity must be registered with an edge hub as edge nodes. This helps in management and monitoring. The new MQTT Sparkplug protocol includes handling the registration of devices, thus streamlining the process.
D002	Edge device data	From streaming video to telemetry data, the big question is: can the data generated by the devices be used as is, or does it need to be aggregated or cleansed? Data transformation was mentioned in one of the edge network ADs. With AI and ML applications deployed on devices, this decision about the handling of data from these devices becomes critical.
D003	Store edge data	In one of the edge cluster ADs, it was mentioned that the decision to store or not store data depends on industry and governmental regulations and auditability reasons. Often, all data from edge devices may not be that useful and probably does not need to be stored. If there is a choice, the solution architect might decide not to store that data because not only does transmitting all the data take time and money, but also, even data storage comes at a price.
	Data security	Data security is described in the AD on security. Suffice it to say that data should be encrypted when stored and when transmitted.

Table 2.7 – Edge device-related ADs

Lastly, we must mention security, specifically edge network security, as an important AD. Security is undoubtedly a key NFR but here, we talk about addressing edge network security. While solution architects should be aware of **zero trust network access** (**ZTNA**) and **secure access service edge** (**SASE**), they must take a holistic approach toward security covering all aspects of the solution, from the cloud to the network to the devices and the applications that run on those devices. ZTNA, SASE and Edge security in general, is covered in great detail in *Chapter 6*.

AD #	Requirement	Factors affecting decision
K001	Edge security	The architect must weigh the cost and challenges of deploying a distributed edge hub topology versus a centralized topology. In the former, a local hub controls a relatively small set of devices – for example, in a store. A centralized topology is where a large edge hub controls a multitude of devices in many remote locations. This is more cost-effective but a riskier design from a security perspective. There is a security feature called **perfect forward secrecy (PFS)** that protects far-edge devices when transmitting data. But data encryption technology should be used so that all data is protected – data in transit and data at rest.

Table 2.8 – Security-related AD

Justifying the decisions made when designing any architecture is important for any solution architect. Many ADs were described in this section, but we are certain there will be more decisions to be made. The important thing is to document all the alternatives, the decision made, and the reason behind it.

Summary

In this chapter, we discussed the main components of an edge architecture. You learned that what makes edge architecture rather unique is the inclusion and heterogeneity of the plethora of edge devices. The typical functional requirements are few, but they are relevant and can be applied to various use cases across a whole lot of industries. We also discussed the different NFRs and their scope.

Lastly, there are many design decisions that solution architects have to make that could be overwhelming. Some of the common ADs were provided more as a starter set. We alluded to the complexity of architecting an edge solution because there are software and hardware components to account for, especially in edge-native designs. This should get architects thinking of the different aspects and domains. In the next three chapters, we will dive into the various architectures from basic to complex and provide recommended practices.

Part 2:
Solution Architecture
Archetypes in Context

We have found that most solutions and patterns in edge computing seem to fit three specific approaches, with slight variations and modifications. We thus refer to these approaches as pattern archetypes. The three chapters in this section will explore and delve into the three main archetypes. These chapters are meant to build successively on the patterns and concepts introduced in previous chapters, so *Chapter 4* builds on the concepts of *Chapter 3*, and *Chapter 5* on *Chapter 4*. This part will show how the architectural components should be used together, the circumstances and situations that should be embraced or avoided, and how and why they are commonly paired.

This part has the following chapters:

- *Chapter 3, Core Edge Architecture*
- *Chapter 4, Network Edge Architecture*
- *Chapter 5, End-to-End Edge Architecture*

3
Core Edge Architecture

This chapter covers the basic user edge architecture, which tends to focus on managing and enabling IoT-type sensors and smart devices. The subtle differences between this architecture and legacy IoT architectures are highlighted. The use of container technology is common in these edge architectures to accommodate the limited capacity of field-deployed edge devices, even if they don't traditionally support common container engines or Linux distributions.

You will learn about the first of the three archetype patterns: the edge device hub pattern (depicted in *Figure 3.6*), how it improves on legacy IoT architectures, and some common variations and modifications you can make to it.

In this chapter, we will cover the following main topics:

- What is legacy IoT architecture?
- Device configuration
- Edge devices versus edge hub
- Containers
- Disconnected operations

By the end of this chapter, you should have a good idea of how and when to use this approach to migrate existing solutions or when to start with a clean slate. Along the way, you will learn ways in which this approach will bring value by saving time and money.

Suggested pre-reading material

- *Using containers to build applications* (`https://www.docker.com/resources/what-container/`)

- *Learn about WebAssembly (Wasm)* (`https://webassembly.org`)

- *Wasm system interface* (`https://wasmbyexample.dev/examples/wasi-introduction/wasi-introduction.all.en-us.html`)

- *WAIT* (`https://dl.acm.org/doi/10.1145/3498361.3538922`)

- *FIDO Alliance's Device Onboard (FDO) specification* (`https://fidoalliance.org/intro-to-fido-device-onboard/`)

What is legacy IoT architecture?

In this section, we will cover legacy IoT architectures: their purpose, promise, and fundamental drawbacks. You will learn why IoT has provided value to business executives, where it was heading as a natural technological progression before being superseded by edge computing, and reasons why it may not have been adopted as widely as initially anticipated.

A bit of history

Large commercial IoT networks became a viable solution for business with the convergence of cheap, low-power embedded processors and inexpensive, ubiquitous cellular data transmission. At that point, it became less expensive to transmit data from sensors than to have humans visit the sensors and record the data manually. However, the data was still tabulated and stored in central locations – a **data center** (**DC**) or, eventually, the cloud.

That approach and those needs formed the basis for initial IoT architectures, which connected devices over transmission networks directly to data processing and storage facilities. We'll cover the initial variations that evolved as precursors to edge computing in a series of three diagrams.

In the first example, rudimentary IoT devices communicated over the internet using cellular data connections directly to an IoT hub for aggregation, processing, and storage. Data was not filtered, reformatted, or otherwise modified until it entered the IoT hub. It was the responsibility of the IoT hub to understand the native protocols and data formats used by the IoT devices and the device locations and to reformat the data while enriching the records with external data sources before sending the results off to other applications for reporting and storage (*Figure 3.1*):

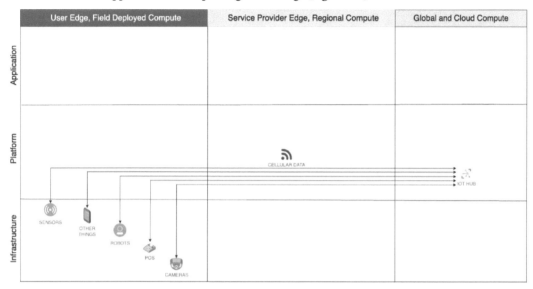

Figure 3.1 – IoT devices backhauling data to an IoT hub over cellular radio

This gave great flexibility in device placement, and typically a 15- to 25-mile transmission range. But it correspondingly required all of the devices to use the same technology and possibly the same mobile **service provider** (**SP**).

In the second example, IoT devices began using a variety of connections and transport types, including Wi-Fi, Bluetooth, and **NarrowBand-IoT** (**NB-IoT**). Additionally, some IoT devices began using **publish/subscribe** (**pub/sub**) brokered protocols such as **Message Queuing Telemetry Transport** (**MQTT**) instead of proprietary or industry-specific protocols. This necessitated the introduction of an IoT router that could support incoming signals and route them over the internet. At the same time, the routers could also package and/or reformat the data into a standard format. The IoT router thus allowed the IoT hub to gradually offload functionality edgeward (*Figure 3.2*):

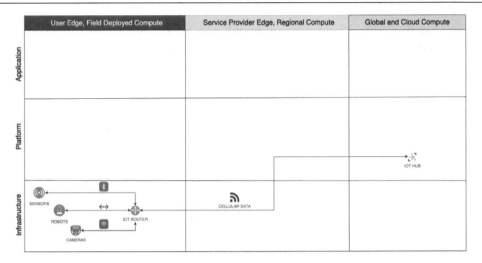

Figure 3.2 – IoT devices sending mixed-format messages to IoT routers, then to an IoT hub

A fundamental drawback to using an IoT router was that the transmission types were mostly shorter-range technologies with Bluetooth in the 6- to 25-foot range, Wi-Fi in the 10- to 150-foot range, and LoRa over 9 miles in optimum conditions. This allowed flexible placement within a defined area. The trade-off was the flexibility gained by supporting heterogeneous transmission options.

In the third example, smartphones provided the ability to perform the duties of both IoT router and IoT hub when powered by cloud provider-specific SDKs and when communicating northbound to proprietary interfaces in cloud services. This emerging trend reduced costs by using **commercial off-the-shelf (COTS)** technology and by leveraging existing cloud-native development skills (*Figure 3.3*):

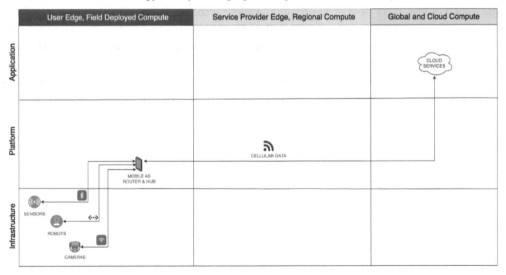

Figure 3.3 – IoT devices connected to mobile devices operating as local IoT hubs

As the preceding three diagrams depict, IoT solutions evolved to migrate supporting platforms southbound toward IoT devices as hardware became cheaper, new protocols and transmission options became supported, and cloud-native development practices emerged. However, IoT devices stubbornly remained single-purpose fixed-function, still needed to connect to a gateway of some sort, and still transmitted raw data northbound to the cloud (backhaul) where all processing, reporting, alerting, and storage were performed by cloud-based services.

Purpose and promise

IoT devices are defined by their capabilities: they are standalone devices that contain functionality consisting of one or more sensors, actuators, or displays/gauges, can connect to the internet (usually wirelessly), and may be IP-addressable. This distinguishes them from peripherals that *must* be connected to a host (computer), use a device driver, and are only usable when connected. IoT devices can be a fixed function and not updatable by the end user, or they may run custom firmware or even an embedded **operating system** (**OS**) capable of loading and running applications.

Prior to IoT device availability, each device would need to be connected directly to a host machine on a local network using a wired connection that was then connected to an uplink for data backhaul. Embedding wireless connectivity into IoT devices allowed them to bypass the host requirement, and sometimes local network requirements, and connect directly to the internet.

This ability to connect directly to the internet simplified deployment architecture complexity and expense, and reduced maintenance costs by removing the need for local IT staff in some situations. Direct connectivity also allowed remote access to devices, eliminating the need for dispatching humans on-site to monitor and maintain the devices. Since on-site personnel were no longer needed, it decreased the cost of operating a fleet of devices, increased the ability to scale the size of fleets of devices, and also increased the quality and quantity of data being collected, the effectiveness of the devices, and the range of possible products that could be created based on these new skills.

Fundamental drawbacks

While IoT devices brought value to the organizations that deployed them, those deployments were not without trade-offs. The drawbacks of this approach were the expense of the data connections and the configuration of the data links, limits to the data transmission speeds, and a lack of standards for the data being transmitted, thus requiring standardizing on a single vendor and/or product (thus requiring vendor lock-in) or maintaining a solution at the receiving end that would catch the data transmission and convert it into a standard format and schema (thus increasing the cost of maintenance).

Device configuration

In this section, we will cover the device configuration use case as an introduction to the edge device hub archetype pattern. You will learn the role and purpose of the infrastructure, platforms, and applications (collectively referred to as *architectural elements* going forward and shown in *Figure 3.4*) that support device operation at the edge. We will briefly discuss the benefits and drawbacks of placement decisions.

Rationale

The device configuration use case is meant to supplant legacy IoT architectures that connect fixed-function devices and embedded systems directly to a host in the cloud. Having a single platform for all devices puts the burden of device registration, protocol support, data collection, and analytics on one platform in one location. However, this approach required all data to be sent to the cloud if it wasn't discarded, resulted in delayed analysis (thus delayed reaction times due to latency), and incurred data transfer and storage expenses. It could also force lock-in to a particular product suite, implementation library or SDK, vendor, or cloud. Some solutions had scalability issues, and costs increased linearly with scale. The advent of edge computing and the new architectures that it introduced mitigated every one of those issues. Let's cover the individual elements with an eye toward what an edge-native approach would entail. The next subsections will explain the elements depicted in *Figure 3.4* and their purpose:

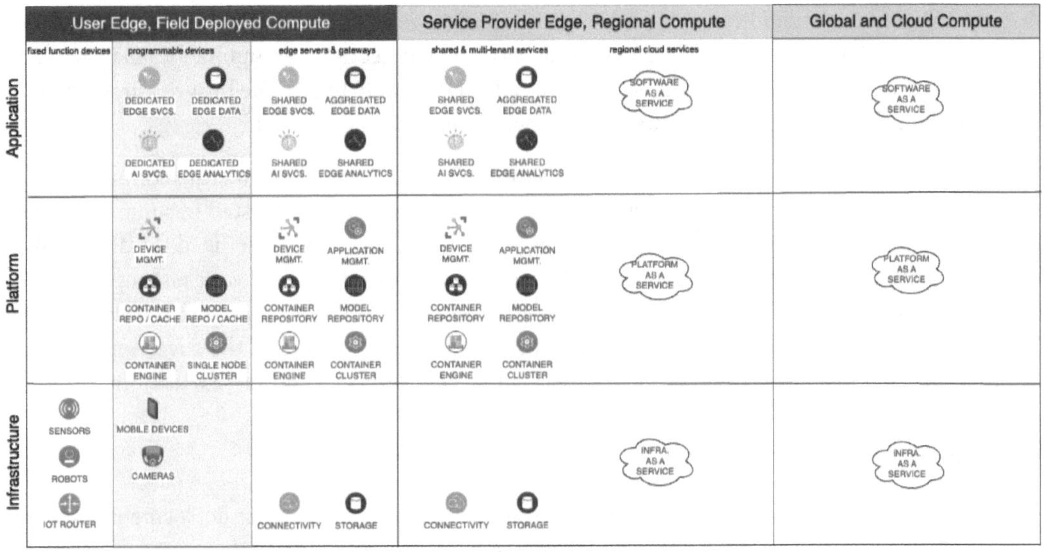

Figure 3.4 – Architectural elements for the edge device hub archetype pattern

Architectural element categories

Let's begin looking at the preceding diagram, starting with the columns moving from left to right. The major columns are for the user edge, the SP edge, and the cloud. The major rows are divided into common cloud layers of applications, platforms, and infrastructure. This grid of rows and columns allows you to observe elements by purpose and simultaneously compare and contrast groups of elements with those in similar locations or those with a similar purpose.

Starting at the top left, the sub-categories of the user edge are:

- **Fixed-function or constrained devices**, which contain single-purpose hardware that cannot run containers
- **Programmable devices**, which contain hardware that supports Linux host machines and devices capable of running container images
- **Edge servers and gateways**, which typically provide shared services, capabilities, and functionality to all hosts and devices in a facility or deployment locality

Next, in the top center, the sub-categories of the SP edge are:

- **Shared and multi-tenant services**, which provide shared services, capabilities, and functionality to multiple locations in a region. They may also provide cross-region failover, additional scalability for local solutions that the user edge may not have, and burst-to-region capabilities from the user edge.
- **Regional cloud services**, which may provide **Infrastructure-as-a-Service (IaaS)**, **Platform-as-a-Service (PaaS)**, and **Software-as-a-Service (SaaS)** solutions, especially to locations with regional or other geography-imposed requirements.

Last, in the top-right column, global and cloud compute provide bare-metal, managed services, and **as-a-Service (aaS)** solutions.

The categories are sometimes overlapping, may sometimes have gaps, and will not be exhaustive. They are meant to be easy to understand, clearly indicate best practices, and illustrate an approach that will likely lead to successful software architecture outcomes. As such, it may not accommodate all edge and corner cases.

User-edge elements

Let's take a more detailed look at the architectural elements listed in each of the categories falling under user edge. We will discuss specific elements, options, and rules of thumb.

Constrained devices

Beginning with the fixed-function devices category, there are no applications or platforms listed since applications and platforms are software-based solutions, and this category is about hardware-imposed constraints. Moving to infrastructure, you'll notice that there are a few items shown. That is because there are many types of devices in this category and those shown are only representative in nature.

The functional types of IoT devices are display, sensor, actuator, emitter, transmitter, receiver, controller, processor, and some combinations thereof. The devices may have their functionality hardwired or fixed, be updatable to some extent, and be programmable to some extent.

> **Rule of thumb**
>
> It is important to note that if an IoT device can host the services supporting an application, it is de facto an edge computing device and considered programmable or dynamic, not fixed function, in nature. A microcontroller, for example, cannot do that.

The best placement decisions for these IoT devices are as close to where they need to be used as possible. Considerations should include determining if the device in question should be placed in the location permanently, if it may need to move occasionally, if it needs to be relocatable on demand, if it has environmental requirements, and if it has a range of movement or is otherwise mobile or articulated.

Programmable devices

In this category, the applications, platforms, and infrastructure should be dedicated only to the needs of the device and possibly any southbound connected or managed fixed-function devices. This is because programmable devices are either dedicated to a specific task or could be otherwise constrained and are not suitable to also function as a server running shared services.

Therefore, our recommendation is to never run shared services on programmable devices unless that device's express purpose is to be a server appliance. Examples of that exception – a programmable device that is also a server appliance – would be a hard drive designed to be a file and/or media server, and an edge appliance designed for and dedicated to managing a fleet of fixed-function devices. Likewise, services on the devices are likely to be stateless.

Beginning in the applications row, programmable devices will likely be required to run applications and services of all types ... whatever the purpose of the device required. That means that it will be rare that the applications on the device will be limited to a single role or type. The diagram depicts applications related to services, data storage, **artificial intelligence** (**AI**), **machine learning** (**ML**), and analytics processing. It makes the most sense to run all required applications on the device itself unless the available storage and processing resources do not permit this.

> **Rule of thumb**
>
> Keep in mind that not all applications need to be running at all times, so consider if you should schedule some to be run based on when they are needed. This will also determine if you need to use an application management solution that permits time-based, location-based, and mobility status or mode-based execution constraints.

In the platforms row, you will find device management, caches and repositories, and container execution environments. Again, these are the most common platforms to be needed for the edge device hub pattern.

The device management element may be a gateway capable of protocol conversion that provides device protocol support, communication, and translation. It could provide device management support including firmware deployment and system telemetry. It could also enable data filtering, a rules engine for events and alerts and complex data transformations, as well as ML model support for data insights and analytics.

It is unlikely that you will have an application management solution running on the device itself, but you may have an application management agent performing some of those duties.

Regarding container and model repositories, there are three options to consider depending on your needs and requirements. First and simplest, you may have a local (or even embedded) repository that is populated by a deployment pipeline. This is only useful if you have a handful of deployment targets that are usually continually connected to the internet. Second, you could have a local repository that is automatically populated by an application or model management system when it retrieves assets from an authoritative remote repository. This is helpful for situations when the device loses connectivity if the management system is configured to check the local repository first or as an automated failover. Third, you may have a caching proxy that impersonates the remote repository. This approach would allow you to create a pyramid structure of caches and repositories for extreme scalability. Or, you could replicate assets horizontally between peered repositories locally or regionally.

For container execution environments, you would likely have Docker or Podman to run containers locally. Some approaches may call for standardizing all environments on the K8s API, in which case you should consider lightweight K8s options such as K3s, KubeEdge, and MicroShift. But even so, Kubernetes clusters have significant overhead requirements and incur a performance penalty over container engines. Note that there are also tools that bridge the gap between the two layers, such as Eclipse ioFog, which uses the Docker runtime locally but can integrate with a remote K8s cluster.

In your container environments, consider how you will connect to individual devices. Initiating outbound connections is preferable since allowing inbound connections to a device increases the potential attack surface. To do this, you would use an application management solution that employs autonomous agents to manage applications locally in these environments and to periodically poll outbound connections. This approach also ensures resilience because the management solution does not need an active network connection to function. However, mission-critical deployments must utilize **out-of-band management (OOBM)** with a dedicated network, not by sharing the same network used for operations.

In the infrastructure row, you'll find the devices. These devices could be robots, RFID scanners, scales, or lights. Common locations for these devices include residences, offices, roads and infrastructure, commercial buildings, factories, in vessels, and on other craft.

Edge servers and gateways

In this category, servers host edge services, AI services, and analytics for multiple edge devices at that deployment location. Any data collected on the server is usually aggregated rather than stored separately to allow reporting on the facility or location as well as sub-units/floors/buildings/sections or individual devices or rooms.

Edge services placed on servers may be stateful, so consider using onboard or local, rather than remote, storage to increase resiliency and decrease latency.

In the platforms row, the device management solution covers the management of fixed-function as well as programmable devices and is the ideal location for both. The server class of edge devices would be expected to be sized to handle any potential growth in the number of deployed devices as well as any increase in running supporting services for those fleets.

Similarly, the server is the ideal location for field-deployed application management services. The server is expected to have both the capacity to run the application management platform and high bandwidth and throughput with low latency, which is ideal for the task. This may also allow the platform to continue running in situations where the local network is physically separate from the internet connection and in situations where the northbound connectivity is unreliable. However, if there are no local edge servers capable of running the application management platform, the SP edge may be the next best location for it.

For model and container repositories, an edge server located on-premises would be the best location for the purposes of latency, resiliency, and suitability. Since each deployment location or edge facility has unique attributes such as geography, purpose, and even governance/regulations, application configuration, ML models, and even, potentially, applications themselves may differ from those stored at other locations and thus require a separate repository instance.

In your container execution environments, you will likely require a multi-node Kubernetes cluster if your edge server capacity allows. This can be implemented on a single machine with each node in a separate **virtual machine** (**VM**), or on separate physical machines for optimum **high availability** (**HA**) and resiliency. This ability to run multiple copies of services on separate cluster nodes is another benefit of the edge server class of machines and ensures the availability of critical locally hosted services. Without this capability, services hosted locally on programmable devices would either lose functionality when a local service went down or would have to add complexity by implementing a solution whereby one device could fail over to a similar service on a nearby device (assuming that the services are fungible and not custom to each device).

In the infrastructure row, you will find connectivity and storage. The storage in this tier should be used primarily for data sharing between devices, for backups and **disaster recovery** (**DR**), and for archiving. Any specialty storage solutions, such as a data historian, would likely belong in the platforms row above and more likely at the SP edge rather than field deployed. Please note that we are using generalities here, and there are always exceptions, especially in cases of extreme scale or vertical specialties.

The connectivity shown here is assumed to be software-based (**software-defined networking**, or **SDN**). The connectivity provided could be in the form of an edge gateway device that features protocol conversion. In many commercial deployments such as a big-box retailer or distribution center, or industrial deployments such as large factories, the connectivity may include private LTE or 5G enabling solutions. In farms and outdoor settings, it may include mesh networks and LoRaWAN installations and support. At stadiums, it can include complete telephony deployments, although those particular locations may rightly be considered satellite locations in the SP edge.

Wrapping up this category, it is important that we mention that edge server deployments do not always have a fixed placement. The deployment locations may have mobility and could include vehicles, boats, and satellites. The **Mayflower Autonomous Ship** (**MAS**) is a good example of an unmanned vessel with a few constrained edge servers (see more about it at `https://mas400.com/`). The MAS is a floating sensor platform operated by constrained programmable edge servers running services in a container engine. The field-deployed edge elements are shown in *Figure 3.5*. For a more complete view, see *slide 6* (*Solution Architecture Details*) from a presentation of the *Open Horizon* open source project at `https://wiki.lfedge.org/display/LE/2020+Fall+Kickoff+Virt ual+Event+Series?preview=%2F29892870%2F29906467%2FMayflower+LF+E dge+2020-10-01+v2_compressed.pdf`:

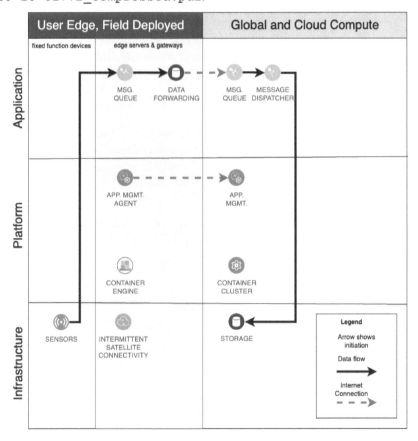

Figure 3.5 – MAS edge solution architecture partial view

An important point to note from the preceding diagram is that there is no benefit to using regional compute over cloud compute resources. Since the boat is sporadically connected to the internet using a low-throughput, high-latency connection, the ability of the cloud to scale and the availability of resources outweigh the potential benefit of additional connection latency differences between boat-to-region versus boat-to-cloud. Additionally, since the boat is traveling, there is no single region that would provide an advantage much of the time.

A second point is that the solution is highly secure. There are no open inbound ports on the vessel. All connections are initiated outbound, and none are kept open for a significant amount of time. This is possible because, other than the mission objectives, all commands are determined, planned, and executed locally on the vessel. And not only are all data connections secured and messages encrypted, but the application management solution also uses **perfect forward secrecy** (**PFS**), which ensures that each session uses new keys.

Edge devices versus edge hub

In this section, we will introduce and cover the edge device hub archetype pattern. We will recommend our preferred order of placement and our reasons for that order, including benefits and drawbacks. We will briefly show how this pattern is applied to some real-world deployments.

> **Note**
>
> An important note before we continue: in this chapter, we do not discuss the network underlay or overlay, topology decisions and optimizations, recommendations, or best practices. For the purpose of focusing on the edge devices and their supporting services, the network is presumed to exist. Later chapters in this book will touch on those matters.

In *Figure 3.6*, we introduce the first archetype pattern. By now, you should be oriented to the style and layout of the chart since we have been building up to it with the previous diagrams:

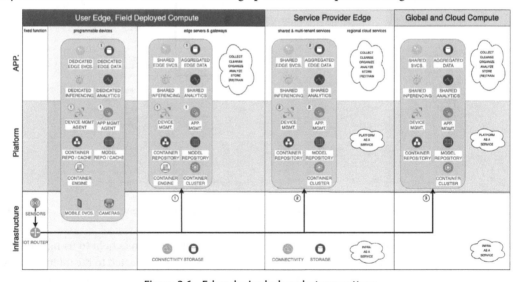

Figure 3.6 – Edge device hub archetype pattern

Let's delve into the details of *Figure 3.6* and describe the main points of interest while showing how to use it.

Reviewing the pattern

This pattern and the recommendations we make are designed for best performance, resilience, and scalability. They may not always be the least expensive or simplest options to manage, but automation and autonomous solutions will mitigate most management issues and could ultimately make deployments easier to manage by fewer persons while providing more configuration flexibility.

In *Chapter 1*, we discussed the various edges, cloud-out versus edge-in, and the concept of an edge cloud. Building on those discussions, let's discuss the trade-offs between running all workloads on the far edge compared to using edge servers and regional compute as mini clouds with lower latencies than global compute using the edge device hub pattern.

If you have fixed-function devices on-premises, the best option for low-latency data transfer and the quickest surfacing of event notifications would be to perform as much inferencing and analytics in the field as possible. This will also lead to more resilience when you encounter upstream connectivity issues. However, you may not have enough computing capacity, power, or storage at that location. In that scenario, offloading to the SP edge becomes the next best option *unless there are no geographically or topologically proximate regional computing facilities available*. Offloading to the cloud would be the least favorable option overall unless timeliness is not critical and your budget is. Just beware of data egress charges from cloud providers, which could erase any potential savings.

For programmable devices, we recommend performing as much work on the device itself as practical, and then the rest on shared edge servers. In an environment with mixed fixed-function and programmable devices, you may want to weigh the mix of analytics workloads more heavily onto the edge servers while keeping most of the inferencing on the programmable devices for the best outcomes. Device and application management should be placed in the most central location to the devices, with only agents running on the programmable devices unless those devices are designed specifically for that purpose (such as a server appliance that also happens to be a programmable device). Another factor to consider is resiliency. If you must process captured data immediately, the constrained devices will need to perform more of the computation and then buffer the output.

For data storage, we recommend leaving data where it is originally stored/recorded/placed for as long as possible and then archiving locally, then regionally, and then globally, in that order of preference. The reason for this recommendation is based on the twin assumptions that most of this data may not be used and is ultimately too expensive to transfer given its inherent value. Additionally, retaining data close to the source minimizes data privacy and governance risks. In order to best utilize that data, we recommend using a solution that enables dynamic and ad hoc querying and data virtualization from any connected node to any arbitrary group of nodes. For more details on this topic, see *Chapter 6*.

For application management, we recommend using a policy-based, no-code, autonomous solution that initiates connections from the edge devices to the server. This approach will allow flexible and scalable solutions while minimizing any potential attack surface. It also helps to ensure disconnected operations without human intervention. Solutions that use this approach include Open Horizon and RHEL Device Edge coupled with Ansible Pull.

For initial deployments on day 1, we recommend using a solution that supports the FDO specification. See the link in the *Suggested pre-reading material* section at the start of the chapter to learn more. There is also an FDO project at the Linux Foundation that provides a reference implementation. FDO support allows zero-touch provisioning and deployments of most devices while ensuring proper device ownership and attestation.

Last, for those interested in edge computing in contested environments, the preceding recommendations should also serve as a solid foundation for tactical edge deployments.

Self-propelled inspection robot example

The following real-world site inspection example solution uses a self-propelled robot – Spot from Boston Dynamics. The solution uses the edge device hub pattern and spotlights the strengths of this approach. Note that the portion of the solution running on the edge server could also run in the SP edge or in the cloud, but it is more performant and resilient when run on-premises.

The robot in this example can travel on pre-programmed routes, including climbing stairs and using elevators. It is sophisticated enough to autonomously recognize obstacles and routes around them. It can also recognize humans and yield to them. It can typically complete an inspection mission in 30 minutes or less on a single charge. The route takes the robot through areas of the premises without connectivity or with severe signal degradation.

The robot can be outfitted with a sensor and/or manipulator pack and uses an attached "backpack" consisting of a low-power edge server. In this scenario, the robot is used for two tasks: checking on fire extinguishers to ensure proper placement, charge, access, and condition with a standard camera and local inferencing; and inspecting electrical panels with a thermal camera and visual inferencing to detect potential hot spots. If a potential issue is detected with a high degree of certainty, a work ticket will be opened upon restoration of network connectivity. See *Figure 3.7* for a diagram of the solution:

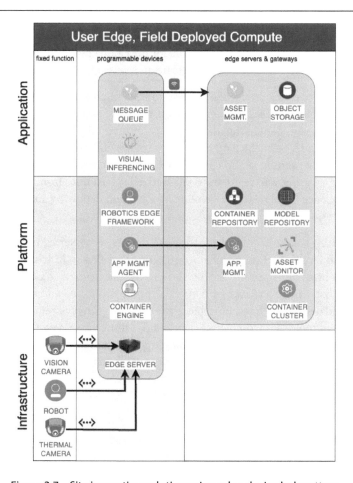

Figure 3.7 – Site inspection solution using edge device hub pattern

You've now seen the archetype pattern, discussed its component elements, and seen an example of a real implementation. Now, let's discuss one of the reasons why edge-native services and applications work so well when deployed to most locations and hardware … containers.

Containers

In this section, we will cover the importance of using containers when developing applications and services. You will learn about how this innovation propelled edge computing to wide adoption. We will briefly discuss serverless computing (AKA cloud functions), and we will touch on the promise of Wasm and the **Wasm System Interface** (**WASI**) for edge computing.

As mentioned in *Chapter 1's Cloud-out versus edge-in* section, software development for edge computing benefitted greatly from the best practices developed for the cloud environment. A large aspect of that benefit was the use of **service-oriented (SO)** software architectures, followed by containerization.

Containerized applications use principles of isolation and abstraction to remove some host and operating system dependencies from the packaged applications that need to run in those environments. This also allows applications with conflicting dependencies to run on the same host without contention. This abstraction from the host enabled an efficient use of system resources superior to some native applications and to those running in VMs. But arguably the best consequence of this approach is the simplicity of placing, running, and removing containerized applications from host machines. A close second-best consequence is the relative ease of developing and deploying applications that support multiple architectures.

Building and supporting software for fixed-function IoT devices, also referred to as embedded systems, has a long list of known pain points. Chief among them, according to Mitch Maiman (https://www.electronicdesign.com/technologies/embedded/article/21165541/intelligent-product-solutions-pain-points-for-embedded-software-design) are limited device resources, unstable drivers, the frequency of required firmware updates, unstable development toolsets, incompatible processors within the same micro-architecture, and a shortage of talented developers. This translates into high operating expenses for the business and a manually intensive development and deployment cycle. With those issues in mind, it becomes easy to see the relative advantages of replacing fixed-function and constrained devices with programmable devices wherever possible.

One emerging solution that marries the ease of development, execution environment, and portability of containerized applications with the ability to run in constrained environments is the Wasm approach. While initially developed for web browsers, Wasm now has several runtimes available for embedded systems that facilitate edge-native software development best practices.

> **Note**
> Alternatively, Rust programs can be compiled into native code and executed on a bare-metal device. This approach provides an alternative to **real-time operating systems (RTOSes)**.

In the near future, we anticipate software development processes allowing containerized application development to generate a single artifact that can be run in both container engines and by Wasm runtimes. Docker has taken the first step in that direction by enabling native Wasm execution within the Docker engine. As a side note, Wasm shows some promise in being a potential technology for powering serverless on the edge, or edge functions, to coin a term.

Serverless computing, or cloud functions, is an approach that uses the sandboxed approach of containers and has applied constraints and trade-offs in order to achieve quick application instantiation. This approach intended to remove the requirement for a persistent application and instead create an ephemeral resource that could be spun up when requested and then immediately removed when finished. As such, serverless applications were intended to be stateless.

When you have a large pool of computing resources available and an expectation of limitless scalability, serverless becomes an inexpensive and efficient way to use those resources. However, the quick instantiation times can strain the less powerful machines sometimes used for edge computing. Edge architectures, especially those not intended for edge servers, have already factored out the requirements of hyper-scalability. Therefore, there is not usually a need for serverless resources in any solutions except those used in edge and enterprise clouds, and those environments are built to handle the demands of serverless computing. As a result, there has been little to no innovation in exploring serverless computing on constrained edge devices.

Disconnected operations

In this section, we will cover unique options and opportunities for not only planning for interrupted network connections but actively planning for those scenarios as an operating requirement. You will learn how some organizations anticipate and respond to those situations in three separate approaches.

In the *Delving into edge-in architectures* section of *Chapter 1*, the first practice listed was *Tolerate interruptions and unavailability of service dependencies and connectivity*. In the edge device hub pattern, you should expect that each individual connection might be unavailable and plan for that eventuality. That may mean planning for devices to lose connectivity to their hub and for performance fluctuations. If that happens, do you plan for the devices to buffer enough untransmitted data, accept the potential data loss, or take some other approach? That may mean that the hub cannot provide the data in response to remote queries or cannot re-transmit the data northbound. It is also important to set expectations regarding the maximum length of time that an outage can occur before unrecoverable data loss happens. Bandwidth, throughput, and latency will vary at any time in the field. This expectation should underpin the architecture.

The *Nexoedge* open source project (`https://lfedge.org/projects/nexoedge/`) is designed for scenarios where partial network outages may occur to remote storage. By storing partial copies of the data in separate locations, you ensure that all data will still be available even if connectivity is interrupted in one of those remote locations. The drawbacks to this approach are that the data is not local, and thus retrieval will incur data transmission costs and latency, and that it is still vulnerable to a full network outage.

The *AgriRegio* project (`https://agriregio.peasec.de/`) uses an approach it calls an "offline-first principle" and designs systems and applications to function without any connectivity as its primary mode of operation. All usage, storage, and connections to remote sensors operate without an internet connection. The only functionality that is not present in those scenarios is installing or upgrading applications, and any optional northbound data transmission.

The *Liquid Prep* open source project (`https://github.com/Liquid-Prep`) creates an ad hoc network mesh using any capabilities present in each device to forward messages to a local hub. The mesh does not require any member to be connected to the internet, and each member can store a few days' worth of data while disconnected. Once connectivity is restored to the hub, accumulated messages are passed along. If the outage lasts longer than the available storage, the **first in, first out** (**FIFO**) queue removes the oldest messages first.

In general, assume that connectivity will not always be present. And if possible, build applications and architectures that do not break when connectivity is removed. For more discussion on this topic, see *Chapter 6*.

Summary

In this chapter, we covered the edge device hub architecture pattern for managing and enabling IoT-type sensors and smart devices and discussed the impacts of placement trade-off decisions. We showed how containerized applications are key in these edge architectures and touched on the role serverless applications could play. You should also have an idea of how you zero-touch deploy edge applications on day 1.

In the next chapter, we will dive into the SP edge and discuss how edge computing affects network overlays and **communication SPs** (**CSPs**).

4
Network Edge Architecture

Communication service providers (**CSPs**) and telcos are mostly interested in network edge solutions because they offer them a way to monetize their investments in 5G infrastructure. While CSPs have built their business on operating physical networks tied to specific geographies, telcos realize that they have access to the same public cloud infrastructure as every other business. That is significant because we will see in this chapter that software is being used to define networks, especially in the era of 5G and beyond.

In *Chapter 3*, we described the basic edge architecture. In this chapter, we will explore network edge architectures and learn how they address, among other features, security and reliability, latency considerations, and storage constraints. The new paradigm is to place compute power at the network edge, thus making it possible to intelligently manage workload placement. The main topics that will be covered are as follows:

- **Network functions virtualization** (**NFV**)
- **Software-defined networking** (**SDN**)
- Underlay and overlay networks
- Network traffic management
- **Multi-access edge computing** (**MEC**)
- Network edge architecture
- Sample architectures

We see that CSPs want to become **digital SPs** (**DSPs**) because hyperscalers are starting to offer software-based network services via cloud-native functionality. This is forcing CSPs to embrace cloud and virtualization as they think about offering new types of 5G and edge computing services.

Definitions

From a **network function** (**NF**) to a DSP, a few definitions are in order before proceeding.

One or more communication connections between different computing devices comprise a network. An NF, as we know it, is the transmission of data between those physical devices while adhering to certain rules. For instance:

- Distribution of data to a pool of servers by a load balancer is an example of an NF

- Filtering of data and deciding which data is safe to consume by a firewall is another example of an NF

As the name suggests, a **virtual NF (VNF)** is a virtualized version where the NF is implemented using software.

Gartner (`https://www.gartner.com/en/information-technology/glossary/csp-communications-service-provider`) defines a CSP as someone who offers telecommunications services leveraging the landline or wireless network infrastructure. While CSP is a generic term, you will hear **internet SP (ISP)**, which provides internet services, or **telecommunication SP (TSP)**, which also offers cable and satellite services.

A DSP is the next step in the evolution of a CSP, whereby companies deliver digital content over the network. Examples of such online services are Apple Music, Spotify YouTube, and so on, and iTunes or Amazon Music are examples of digital stores where people can access digital content.

NFV

Let's take a short trip down memory lane. Media gateways, routers, **home location registers (HLRs)**, **IP Multimedia Subsystem (IMS)**, and so on were components that made up legacy telecom systems. Customized hardware, operating systems, and other software were required to offer telecom services to customers. These legacy network devices were very expensive and had high operating costs. Therefore, customers ended up with high **operating expenses (OPEX)** and **capital expenses (CAPEX)**. That resulted in a lock-in with long-term contracts with the telcos for support and maintenance. Another byproduct of such environments was that scalability came at a premium and self-healing capability was minimal or non-existent.

IP-based technologies gradually replaced legacy networks, to the point where even legacy services such as voice (phone) communications are now delivered over IP (VoIP). This led to the ubiquitous wireless data networks of today, of which 5G is the latest incarnation. Telcos started prioritizing the adoption of cloud-native computing. That was a paradigm shift by the **network equipment providers (NEPs)** to offer VNFs. These are virtualized versions of legacy **physical NFs (PNFs)** designed to run in **virtual machines (VMs)** or containers on commodity hardware. Such virtualization using software leads to agile networks, provides scalability, self-healing, and closed-loop assurance, and comes with significant OPEX and CAPEX savings.

NFV, although very similar and often used interchangeably with VNF, refers to the running of SDN functions on commodity hardware. This network virtualization initiative has been led by some of the world's biggest telecom operators.

Carrier network

A carrier network is a rather complex system that connects various network devices to transmit data from one location to another. One of the main challenges for network vendors is maintaining their **service-level agreements** (**SLAs**). Carrier networks are being transformed by NFV because it helps vendors maintain their SLA guarantees.

The NFV specification is managed by the **European Telecommunications Standards Institute** (**ETSI**). A standard diagram showing the VNF and NFV layers is depicted in *Figure 4.1* (*Source*: `https://www.etsi.org/technologies/nfv`):

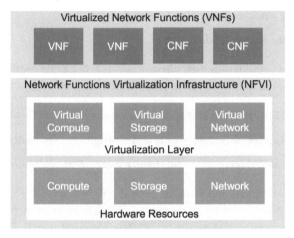

Figure 4.1 – NFV and VNF layers

Note

ETSI is an independent non-profit standards organization in the field of information and communications.

There are three layers in this network edge platform architecture, starting from the bottom: hardware resources, virtualization layer, and virtualized functions. They have to do with decoupling. The NFV decouples NFs from the hardware, which could be proprietary, and runs them as software. Other functions such as firewalls, traffic control, and virtual routing are run as VNFs.

The VNFs are deployed as VMs running Linux on commercial hardware. The traditional network appliances that might be running on proprietary hardware are also known as PNFs. You also see boxes named **CNF**. These are cloud-native NFs, which are containerized versions of VNFs.

Two other important areas in an NFV architecture are not described here because they are not that relevant to edge computing – namely, **management and orchestration** (commonly referred to as **MANO**), and **operations and business support systems** (**OSS/BSS**).

Source: https://www.ibm.com/cloud/architecture/architectures/network-automation

NFV considerations

At a high level, the different classes of NFV workloads as put forth by ETSI are:

- **Data-plane workloads**: Related to packet handling
- **Control-plane workloads**: Related to session management, routing, or authentication
- **Signal processing workloads**: Related to digital processing
- **Storage workloads**: Related to disk storage

Organizations have strong controls over their physical network, but when considering an NFV solution, architects must pay attention to their security posture. At a minimum, look at these three areas:

- **Data encryption**: Encrypt data in storage, when transmitted, and when in use
- **Security key management**: Securely store and manage keys associated with data encryption
- **Access control**: Establish access controls to all aspects of the virtual network

We have talked about cloud-native and virtualization of NFs but not in the same breath. Since it was introduced in 2012, applying NFV principles to core network infrastructure has led to more agile and cost-efficient network deployments. However, these VNFs have traditionally been implemented using VMs. The question quite often asked by hyperscalers is, *Can it all run in containers?* In *Figure 4.1*, we even depicted **cloud-native network functions** (**CNFs**), and while the move to containerize VNFs has started, certain telecom applications require very high-performing networks in terms of throughput, and latency and telcos are taking their time to create containerized versions of their services. Another subtle but important reason is that VMs have been proven to be more secure in networking topologies when compared to containers because of the isolation provided by hypervisors at a system level. One advantage of VMs is that they provide better integration with hardware. This is critical for data acquisition and processing, for example. Containers abstract the underlying hardware, which makes them more portable but less integrated. To understand the difference between VM and container security, check out this URL: https://www.techtarget.com/searchsecurity/tip/Container-vs-VM-security-Which-is-better.

SDN

As the term implies, software is used to provide NFs. It is done by using **application programming interfaces** (**APIs**) to communicate with network hardware and direct network traffic over a virtual overlay network. SDN aims to bring the benefits of cloud computing to network deployment and the management of networks by delivering them as code.

The devices, such as a router or switch, in a traditional network are only aware of the status of the network device next to it. SDN, on the other hand, can manage all the devices because of the centralization of network control.

Simply put, companies are using SDN because it's a way to efficiently control network traffic and can be scaled as needed. SDN separates the control plane (that is, routing and packet forwarding functions) from the data plane (that is, underlying infrastructure). The brain of the SDN network is the centralized SDN controller, which offers a secure network since network administrators can set access policies from a central location across the entire network. The AI technology built into SDN controllers can detect periods of high network utilization and when they occur. Based on that, the SDN controller can request more processing be completed at the edge to alleviate network bottlenecks.

Without going into the details, it suffices to know that there is one component, the SDN controller, that is central to SDN architecture. See *Figure 4.2*, which also depicts three layers – the application layer, the control layer, and the data layer:

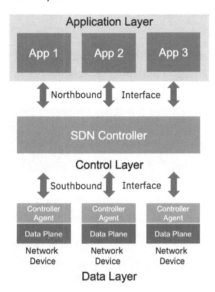

Figure 4.2 – SDN topology layers

The **data layer** is also known as the **infrastructure layer**. The northbound interface is typically a REST API or a web interface that lets the user or application layer communicate with the SDN controller, while the southbound interface allows the SDN controller or the control layer to interact with the network devices.

Because the SDN controller is centralized, it could be a potential **single point of failure** (SPOF). A solution architect has to be aware of that when designing an SDN solution topology.

VNF, NFV, SDN, and edge computing

A VNF is not directly related to edge computing, but it helps in supporting emerging use cases such as AR/VR and image processing at the regional/network edge. Introducing VNFs at the edge of the network and near the end users is beneficial because it reduces end-to-end latency, accelerates **time to response (TTR)**, and, most importantly, mitigates unnecessary utilization of the core network.

We saw how SDN, by way of the SDN controller, helps with cost-efficient networking and direct network management. That in turn could help improve efficiency and reduce latency in the realm of edge computing. SDN complements NFV because NFV moves services to a virtual layer and SDN helps control data packet routing through centralized management functions.

Underlay and overlay networks

After all the talk about NFV and SDN, it behooves us to briefly describe underlay and overlay networks. This concept seems to follow the software engineering principle – solve any problem by introducing an extra level of indirection.

Very simply put, an **underlay network** is the underlying physical infrastructure of the network. An **overlay network** is a virtual logical network constructed on top of an underlay network using virtualization (see *Figure 4.3*):

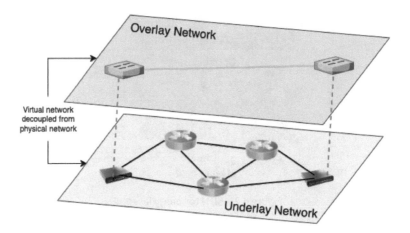

Figure 4.3 – Overlay and underlay networks

Routers, switches, firewalls, and servers are devices found in an underlay network, which are interconnected via routing protocols. In an overlay network, which is software-based, data is transmitted via virtual links. *Chapter 9* compares the security aspects of underlay and overlay networks. Suffice it to say that overlay networks provide segmentation and isolation, which helps with security. They also simplify the management of network devices by providing more granularity to apply policies.

From an edge computing perspective, the overlay network has relevance because it provides a path to create logical networks that could be leveraged by applications and, especially, edge devices. This way, the overlay network can connect to thousands of devices more quickly since interaction with the physical network is not required and network administrators are not constrained by the physical network.

Network traffic management

Speaking of networks, the question every telco wants to know is if they are meeting their SLA commitments. That is where network traffic reporting and management come into play. It is a way to determine and manage the health of a network by collecting real-time data from all network elements such as routers, switches, and so on, and endpoint devices such as laptops, mobile phones, and more. By monitoring, intercepting, and inspecting network traffic, telcos can direct traffic to an optimum resource based on certain **quality of service** (**QoS**) policies. This helps network administrators to alleviate congestion, reduce latency, and minimize packet loss.

While all these are tasks performed by network administrators, today's networks are too complex to be managed manually. It is made possible by software known as **network management software**, also known as **network management systems**. The network management system uses some standard protocols to automatically collect information from various network devices. This is useful for tasks such as updating software or performance monitoring. Some of the network management protocols used are listed in *Table 4.1*:

Protocol	Description
SNMP	**Simple Network Management Protocol** (**SNMP**) is an open application layer protocol used to monitor the network and detect any network faults. It collects information about managed devices on IP networks for analysis. Examples of devices are routers, switches, cable modems, servers, and more.
ICMP	**Internet Control Message Protocol** (**ICMP**) is a TCP/IP network layer protocol. It is used by network devices, usually routers, to send operational information. It determines if data is reaching the intended destination at the right time.
Streaming network telemetry	Streaming network telemetry is a relatively new protocol that uses a push mechanism to send **key performance indicators** (**KPIs**) from network devices to the network management system. It sends it at a higher rate with lesser impact on the network devices compared to SNMP.

Table 4.1 – Protocols used in network management

Given the components and the protocols used, we could visualize a high-level network management architecture, as shown in *Figure 4.4*:

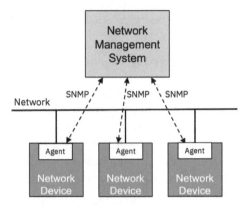

Figure 4.4 – Network management architecture

Network management systems are meant to be the eyes and ears of network administrators. They use AI/ML features to determine patterns in the network traffic flow to assist network administrators with many repetitive but vital tasks:

- Automating network maintenance and software updates

- Monitoring network performance and accelerating troubleshooting

- Identifying security threats

With respect to edge computing, incorporating AI/ML technology into network automation and management helps with the enforcement of network and edge placement policies because they would be based on past and existing network patterns. It can also help with the identification and classification of a multitude of devices on the network. For example, the system can determine if a separate network slice makes more sense to handle network traffic congestion and data loads.

MEC

MEC is a network architecture that brings cloud capabilities to the edge of the network. It was formerly known as **mobile edge computing**. It is where mobile networks and the internet meet and hand off network traffic.

What started out as a concept is now also a `standards framework` developed by `ETSI`. They decided to expand the aperture by replacing "mobile" with "multi-access" because it was no longer just about mobile phones but had to do with the plethora of connected devices. MEC is about making edge devices, including IoT-type devices, smarter by running applications on them and making sense of the data that they generate.

This is where many of the previously described concepts converge. *Figure 4.5* shows MEC positioned within a large edge architecture. As with everything else in the realm of edge computing, MEC is meant to reduce latency and ensure a highly efficient network service delivery in remote places. MEC-related tasks are meant to be performed in real time or near real time:

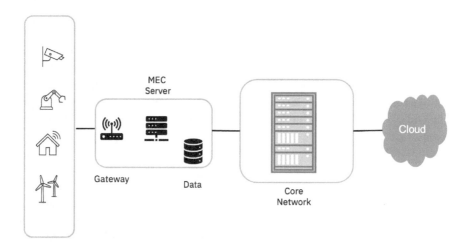

Figure 4.5 – MEC within the larger edge architecture

In the past, mobile applications running in cellular networks were placed in centrally located and serviced large **data centers** (**DCs**). Now, SPs have found good use cases for MEC because they can move workloads and services, which are now decoupled from physical devices, out of the core network to the edge of the network. An example is running workloads at cellular base stations, which are a lot closer to the user. Deploying applications on MEC units and the placement of MEC closer to the edge increases throughput and reduces latency.

MEC plays a key role in many edge solutions because, depending on the use case, it can be deployed in any of these three locations:

- Near the tower or base station that is closest to the end user
- In a central office or regional DC that is relatively the farthest point from the devices or **user equipment** (**UE**)
- Somewhere in between, which can act like a hub location

We will see later in the chapter example scenarios on how mobile operators are introducing 5G services and leveraging the same cloud-native infrastructure to run both MEC and **virtualized radio access networks** (**vRANs**) on the same commodity hardware.

Network edge architecture

The network core, as depicted in *Figure 4.4*, is the infrastructure that runs and supports all the devices in an enterprise's internal network. It is one of two major components in a wireless telecommunication network. The network edge is a collection of servers and devices that connect the company's internal network to the internet. It can be on-premises or in the cloud.

Chapter 3 described the differences between legacy IoT-type architecture and cloud-native architecture. Telcos have a lot of legacy infrastructure and make extensive use of VMs on proprietary hardware in the compute layer. Part of their modernization journey includes the use of container technology running on **commercial-off-the-shelf** (**COTS**) hardware. As they adopt newer technologies, telcos and CSPs see the need to support some existing legacy systems as well as inject new technology. This blend of old and new technologies shows up in network edge architectures. Let's look at some real-world scenarios.

RAN

A RAN is the other major component in a wireless telecommunications system. It connects UE or electronic devices to the network via a radio link. We talked about the virtualization of NFs. The RAN can also be virtualized, and we see that happening more with the advent of 5G technology. A vRAN uses the same virtualization principles whereby the RAN NFs are virtualized and deployed on a containerized cloud platform. *Figure 4.6* shows the virtualization levels in a RAN:

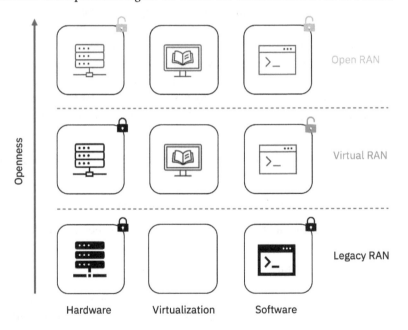

Figure 4.6 – Virtualization in a RAN

In the telcos' network modernization journey, virtualizing RAN functions is key because as with NFV, it makes it easier to use commodity hardware, and because everything is done through software, it is easier to manage and make enhancements. This is in fact the ongoing goal of 5G network transformation. We assume readers are familiar with 5G mobile technology, which at a high level has three main components – RAN, transport network, and core network. See *Figure 4.7*. We will leave the vRAN versus Open RAN debate to the networking experts:

5G Network

Figure 4.7 – 5G network components

Suffice it to say that disaggregation is the goal, coupled with cloud-native and container-based RAN solutions. Disaggregating the hardware from the software gives more freedom to the network operators on how and when to deploy certain technologies and features. It also provides flexibility to their maintenance cycles. It simplifies network operations, lowers costs, and provides greater efficiency when using open architecture.

CSPs and hyperscalers

We have all read about how CSPs are looking for ways to take advantage of new technologies and grow their revenues beyond just connectivity because a lot of it is software-based. From containerization to virtualization, hyperscalers are looking to expand into new areas such as networking. Hence, we see a new partnership of sorts between these two entities. We say that because in this partnership between telcos and hyperscalers, each is lacking a piece of the solution stack. While telcos own the physical network and location, the hyperscalers provide the cloud platform and virtualization techniques.

But hyperscalers recognized the opportunity and have packaged their cloud platforms and tools into managed, turn-key edge cloud infrastructure. With CSPs owning much of the infrastructure real estate, it makes sense for them to partner with hyperscalers. And the beauty of such a partnership is that it can have many-to-many relationships, as shown in *Figure 4.8*:

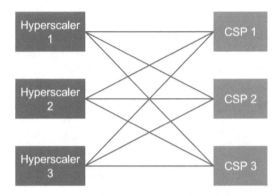

Figure 4.8 – Hyperscaler-to-CSP relationship

While hyperscalers dominate this paradigm, at some point, this partnership could swing in the CSP's favor as they attempt to capture a share of the hyperscaler's revenue by positioning compute and storage resources in various locations in their network. Depending on the industry and the strength of the hyperscaler in a particular geography, a CSP can choose to work with a hyperscaler and with their help offer new telco services to customers in that region. Similarly, a hyperscaler could offer its cloud platform and services to any CSP willing to work with it. It boils down to the vertical opportunity and technical breadth of each player in a region.

Sample architectures

Now, let's look at some sample architectures where the previously described components, technologies, and principles come together. The major components are the network hardware, the virtualization layer, the applications, and the enterprise cloud. *Figure 4.9* is not meant to muddy the waters more but to provide yet another perspective on the various edge realms:

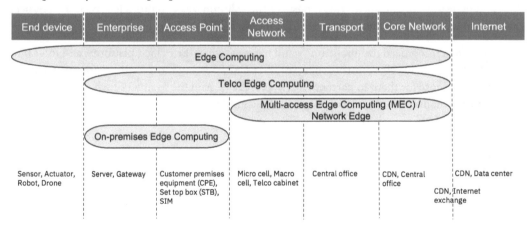

Figure 4.9 – Various edge realms

Note that an **access point** (**AP**) is a term used to describe a network device that allows wireless devices to connect to wired networks. Transport is defined as the network infrastructure providing connectivity to various customer services. It typically connects the RAN and the core network. In the case of 5G, it provides the network slicing function.

> **Note**
>
> In 5G RAN architecture, it is possible to split the two functional units: the **distributed unit** (**DU**), responsible for real-time functions, and the **centralized unit** (**CU**), responsible for non-real-time functions.

Source: `https://www.rcrwireless.com/20200708/fundamentals/open-ran-101-ru-du-cu-reader-forum`

Manufacturing scenario

Industrial manufacturing still relies heavily on **programmable logic controllers** (**PLCs**) and **human-machine interfaces** (**HMIs**). A PLC is a ruggedized industrial computer that is adapted and programmed for the control of manufacturing processes in assembly lines, industrial robots, and other machines. These systems and devices are the workhorses of industrial manufacturing and work really well. However, they depend on proprietary operating systems and are not only expensive to acquire but cost a lot to maintain and upgrade. We should mention that there is now open source PLC software such as PLC4X from Apache Foundation (`https://plc4x.apache.org/`), 4diac from Eclipse (`https://eclipse.dev/4diac/`), and others.

These days, robot controllers that are software-controlled have taken their place and have the ability to control many industrial robots. If you visit a car or an airplane manufacturing company, you will notice many such robots working seamlessly churning out products. There could be many industrial robots in an assembly line in a manufacturing unit. With many such assembly lines in the company, the density of such edge-type devices increases. Programming, management, and control of these devices is critical.

Keeping things functioning smoothly in such an environment requires deploying workloads onto these devices consistently and in a timely manner. One option from the network edge perspective is to employ RAN functional splitting, where the **radio unit** (**RU**) is placed on-premises, and the other RAN components of DU, the **centralized unit** (**CU**), and the network core are deployed in the public cloud:

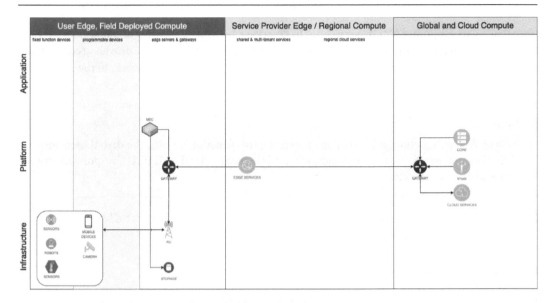

Figure 4.10 – High-level architecture showing MEC and RU on-premises

Additionally, a MEC unit is placed on-premises where the edge application is deployed. A database could also be deployed on-premises to store the data generated by the devices for analysis, as shown in *Figure 4.10*.

In this solution, the focus is on coverage and device density, rather than low latency and high bandwidth. This architecture is favored by enterprises that prefer a low RAN footprint on-premises.

Healthcare scenario

Hospitals typically operate in an environment where every second and minute is precious, hence the need for quick decisions, which translates into low-latency networks. We all remember getting X-rays, and somebody would physically deliver them to a doctor or a specialist for diagnosis. Whether they are X-rays, CT scans, or ultrasounds, these days images are taken and transmitted as electronic files. Often, these large image files are sent to another location in the hospital for diagnosis, and that requires greater bandwidth in the network.

Deviating a bit from the previous solution, one network option is to place all three RAN components – the RU, DU, and the CU – on-premises and keep the network core in the public cloud.

In addition, the CSP could choose to dedicate a 5G network slice for the hospital. The solution architect also has the option to place an MEC unit in or near the hospital premises, which would not only help with faster data access but also maintain the data's security posture. See *Figure 4.11*:

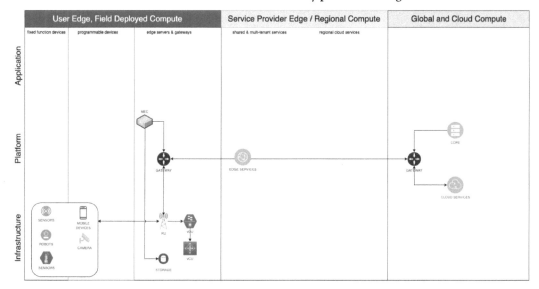

Figure 4.11 – High-level architecture showing MEC and RAN on-premises

It makes sense to deploy the AI/ML application, which is required to help with the identification and analysis of those medical images, on that MEC platform in the hospital. After the image is analyzed, it is often stored within the hospital premises or in a nearby secure repository to comply with regulatory requirements such as the **Health Insurance Portability and Accountability Act** (**HIPAA**) in the US. The solution architect has to think not only about network design but also about other aspects such as storage and data sovereignty.

Campus network scenario

In this scenario, the three RAN components – the RU, DU, and CU, and maybe even the network core – are all deployed on-premises. The advantage of such an architecture is that the customer has full control of the platform and it is secure. See *Figure 4.12*:

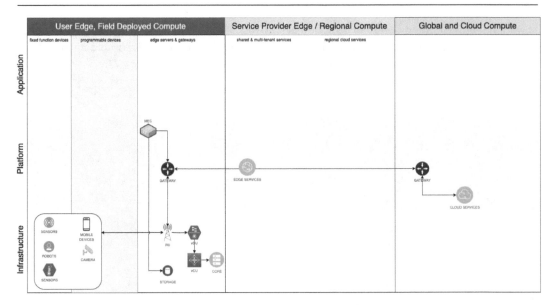

Figure 4.12 – High-level architecture showing MEC, RAN, and network core on-premises

A solution architect can envision such a setup in a stadium where the goal is to create a private campus network for the sole purpose of providing an immersive experience to the spectators. This is done by delivering an AR service in the stadium for the spectators and providing additional data and statistics during the game.

The primary purpose is to distribute video content taken from multiple angles during a live sporting event via multiple 5G-enabled cameras. The captured video is sent through a dedicated 5G network slice to a MEC site for AR processing. Player names, profiles, and statistics are added to the video stream as an AR overlay, and the enriched video is transmitted back to spectators in the stadium in real time.

Such an environment is facilitated by possibly setting up a private 5G network on-premises to support these common edge requirements of coverage at scale, low latency, high bandwidth, and very high device density.

Summary

In this chapter, we discussed the different aspects of network edge architecture. It showed the importance of CSPs needing to adopt cloud and virtualization to offer new services that drive growth and improve customer experience. CSPs are attempting to become DSPs.

We talked about the virtualization of NFs and how it is helping telcos take advantage of cloud-native technologies. You also learned about SDN. We saw the prevalence of network management systems and how they help network administrators.

Finally, we closed the chapter with a description of MEC, which has gained popularity with the advent of 5G technology. Three common edge use cases were described that showed variations in the location of the network components.

In the next chapter, we will look at end-to-end architectures.

5

End-to-End Edge Architecture

Often, we come across solution architectures that encompass every aspect of edge computing, from the enterprise all the way to the far-edge device. *Chapters 3* and *4* laid the groundwork to discuss such end-to-end edge architectures, which include compute nodes of different sizes and capabilities, analytics done at various points, storage options of all the generated data, and, finally, the network. A solution architect has to take into account those macro components plus factor in types of devices and their form factors, the applications that get deployed on the edge devices, management and monitoring options, and security aspects.

You come across such end-to-end edge architectures in many industries, from automotive manufacturing to healthcare to logistics to large retail. What makes such architectures interesting is the kind of data that is generated by the edge devices and the scale of the entire solution.

In this chapter, we will explore some specific industry edge architectures and learn how they integrate existing networks with 5G technology. We will take a look at the following topics:

- IT and OT convergence
- AI and Edge Computing
- Industrial Edge Scenario
- Manufacturing scenario
- Retail edge scenario
- Retail store scenario
- Edge reference architecture
- Edge and distributed cloud computing

IT and OT convergence

IT and OT have always been at odds, and with the push to digital transformation, the roles have overlapped even more, causing more friction. OT is traditionally focused on controlling and monitoring processes in the enterprise, such as in the warehouse or factory shop floor, where they deal with a heterogeneous environment consisting of different types of equipment and devices. IT, on the other hand, deals with a more homogeneous environment of systems and the management of the same.

It is often said IT is about the business, while OT is the business. Security, organizational siloes, and cultural barriers notwithstanding, IT and OT need to work together for the good of the company, especially in this era of digital transformation. For a business to drive efficiency, make productivity gains, and eventually increase profitability, there needs to be IT and OT convergence. In an edge computing paradigm, IT and OT should be the yin and yang of a business. See *Figure 5.1*:

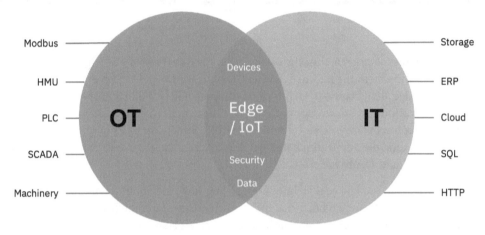

Figure 5.1 – IT and OT convergence facilitated by edge computing

OT brings its vast experience with **supervisory control and data acquisition (SCADA)** systems, **programmable logic controllers (PLCs)**, **hydro-mechanical units (HMUs)**, and **manufacturing execution systems (MES)**. IT understands software and IT-related platforms such as the cloud, databases, **enterprise resource planning (ERP)** tools, and so on. But there are some common components such as edge devices, data, and, above all, security that both teams have to deal with, and that's where we see them needing to work together.

As mentioned, edge and IoT are bringing IT and OT closer. In fact, we can now make the case that there is a lot more convergence and cooperation because applications such as video analytics, health monitoring, logistics tracking, and digital farming deployed on a global network of devices and systems have broken down the perceived walls. From managing these devices and sensors to deploying applications on them, everyone responsible for maintaining security in these environments has forced this convergence of IT and OT. In this digital era, converged IT-OT infrastructure will need to connect with various production-floor machines or warehouse systems or to devices that extend beyond the walls of the traditional **data center (DC)** and deliver analytics, monitoring statistics, and other client-side services to customers in real time. Edge computing provides a common or unified platform for teams to both work in and bring their expertise to solve business problems and demonstrate value within the enterprise and to their external clients.

AI and edge computing

This is yet another type of convergence, that of AI and edge computing. Certain applications, such as autonomous vehicles on the road, healthcare monitoring, and industrial robots in an assembly line, require immediate responses because they do real-time analysis and are faced with making quick decisions. This is where deploying AI algorithms at the edge comes in because it brings intelligent decision-making to the edge and reduces the need to transfer data to central servers.

We talked about deploying AI models to the edge, but the training and retraining of those models are done on the enterprise edge or the regional edge and typically not done at the far edge. Even the deployment and management of these AI models across a large number of edge devices has its own challenges of scale and consistency. Not all devices are created equal, and neither are the AI models. Solution architects must be cognizant of the form factor of the edge devices, the constraints they have, and the size and requirements of the AI models.

The convergence of AI and edge computing is undoubtedly a significant step forward in IoT and real-time decision-making. However, several challenges must be addressed to realize its full potential. The deployment and management of AI models across potentially thousands of edge devices present scalability, consistency, and maintainability challenges. *Figure 5.2* shows the flow of data from the far-edge devices, after inferencing, sent to storage in the layers to the right, and the AI model building and training being done where there is more compute and storage then deployed onto the edge devices:

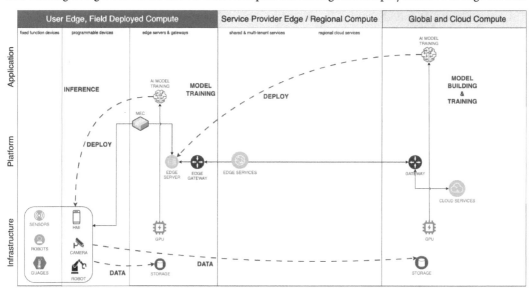

Figure 5.2 – AI model life cycle in edge computing

Inferencing at the edge in real-time or edge analytics in near real time is possible thanks to AI at the edge – specifically, AI applications deployed on the edge devices. The following chapter, *Chapter 6*, talks about dealing with all the data that is generated or collected at the edge. Suffice it to say that a lot of data is required to train AI models, which means all that data has to be stored somewhere, and, as shown in *Figure 5.2*, some of it can be stored in the enterprise edge or it can all be sent for storage in the enterprise cloud.

We would be amiss to not mention the hardware advancements that have played a key role in bringing AI to the edge. Smaller yet more powerful processors are now available that are capable of running complex AI models at a much lower cost. Simultaneously, ML algorithms are more optimized now, and the processing power required for modeling and training fits in the constrained edge devices. Also, model training and pruning techniques are more efficient now, which makes it possible to run these AI algorithms on edge devices.

Solution architects must be mindful of the size of ML models that can be deployed on the devices. Not only do the models have to be small in size, but they have to be so designed that they perform a limited set of AI tasks efficiently. *Chapter 6* talks about using data to build ML models, and *Chapter 8* discusses the deployment operations of these AI models at the edge.

Industrial edge scenario

This scenario was briefly discussed in *Chapter 4*. Many enterprises continue to use 4G or Wi-Fi connectivity within their premises, but many devices rely on wired connectivity. For example, industrial systems continue to use PLCs because they are ruggedized, reliable, and cost-effective. PLCs and **human-machine interfaces** (**HMIs**) are being combined with edge computing technologies to provide better control and analytics. Nowadays, edge controllers, as shown in *Figure 5.3*, are providing PLC functions and more by way of monitoring applications and optimizing energy usage:

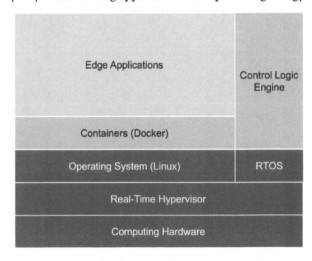

Figure 5.3 – Example edge controller augmenting PLC system

Figure 5.3 shows the components of an edge controller. The traditional control logic engine continues to run on a **real-time operating system** (**RTOS**) because they are very efficient and provide predictable latencies, meaning function calls are guaranteed to return within a specific timeframe. Both RTOS and other OSes, such as Linux, are run on a virtualization layer on purpose-built hardware. Containerized edge applications make up the new software technology that applies to industrial systems to help enterprises offer new services. These controllers allow companies to deploy newer applications and get better insights on the shop floor while continuing to operate on existing underlying automation systems.

Edge controllers work in conjunction with existing PLC systems to optimize assembly-line performance and energy usage and monitor machinery health. From an edge computing perspective, the edge controller is used to gather data and provide additional analytics and visualization, even video, as and when needed.

When it comes to using edge controllers, the subtlety of OT and IT convergence should not be lost on the solution architect here. OT teams, because of their knowledge and experience, will want to continue to have control and decision-making over the hardware used in these edge controllers while they defer software-level decisions to IT.

Source: `https://www.controleng.com/articles/edge-control-evolution/`

Manufacturing scenario

In an effort to make the manufacturing process more efficient, we see assembly-line robots, warehouse robots, acoustic calibrators, and industrial cameras inspecting flaws on the manufacturing line becoming more commonplace in the realm of industrial automation. From an edge computing perspective, these are all edge devices that run applications specific to the tasks they perform. We will look at a scenario that uses AI to detect anomalies or flaws in robotic welding, with the ultimate goal of preventing assembly-line stoppage. Typically, such quality checks are done manually by the **quality control** (**QC**) team, which adds time delays and could be costly.

The four groups of components in this scenario are:

- The devices, including robotic welding components and ruggedized cameras on the shop floor
- The edge-related platform components in the enterprise
- 5G networking components and software
- Services in the enterprise cloud

Enterprises have different options when it comes to networking. They can work with **communications service providers** (**CSPs**), partner with telcos, or get all the services from a hyperscaler. Before going any further into the architecture, we want to point out that there are two deployment options when it comes to rolling out 5G – public and private. *Table 5.1* lists the characteristics of public 5G and private 5G without getting into the minutia:

Category	Public 5G	Private 5G
Consumer of network	Public 5G wireless networks offer the same level of service and security to all customers, businesses, and consumers that are on the network, other than slicing. We will refer to the public network as being owned by a mobile network operator (MNO), also referred to as a CSP. In the case of the public 5G network, the 5G spectrum is owned by the MNO/CSP, and the management of the network and service is also their responsibility.	Private 5G wireless networks are operated privately by a group, a company, or government agencies. They create a more secure wireless experience and are protected at busy times. Some examples where private 5G networks are deployed are manufacturing facilities, retail locations, shipping ports, airports, hospitals, defense bases, and so on that require secure, predictable performance.
Security and isolation	The security risk is higher and comes from the public sharing the network. Also, when the network is busy, it could impact all users equally.	These networks are the most secure because there is connectivity to the public network and the enterprise has full control of it.
Size of the network	These networks are typically built to serve millions to hundreds of millions of subscribers, hence the scale is many times larger than private networks. The design and deployment of these networks are much different than with private 5G networks.	The networks are typically small and deployed in one or more locations of an enterprise, and can be owned and operated by the enterprise, or can be deployed and managed by systems integrators (SIs) and managed SPs (MSPs).
Integration	It is a distributed architecture when deploying public 5G networks on a hybrid cloud platform.	Private 5G networks can be isolated from the public 5G network, or some enterprises may integrate with the public network of MNO/CSP for mobility and roaming outside the enterprise location/campus.

Table 5.1 – Characteristics of public 5G and private 5G

In this particular instance, we have chosen to describe the option where the auto manufacturing company has decided to work with a hyperscaler for all its 5G networking needs. They have decided to set up a private 5G environment on-premises where along with the **centralized unit** (**CU**), the **distributed unit** (**DU**) and **radio unit** (**RU**) are the 5G core. Hence, there are no components in the SP column and no tasks, per se, for the CSP. See *Figure 5.4*, which depicts the topology of the proposed solution:

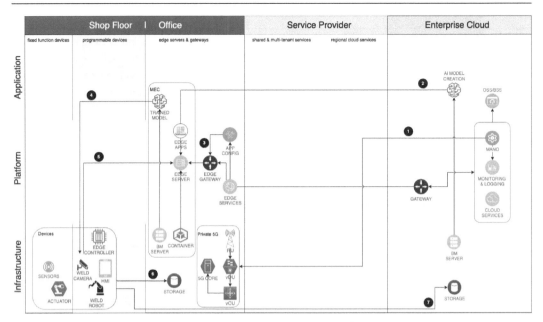

Figure 5.4 – Edge solution architecture in a manufacturing scenario

The architecture flow is explained in *Table 5.2*. The numbers correspond to those depicted in *Figure 5.4*.

No.	Description
1	The network management layer is multi-tenanted and hosted by the hyperscaler in the enterprise cloud. Management and network operations (MANO) plus tasks related to operations support systems (OSS) and business support systems (BSS) are all handled by the hyperscaler from the enterprise cloud, which is the "managed from" location. As mentioned earlier, the private 5G on-premises network provides a secure network for use by all devices in the enterprise.
2	Initial ML model creation and training require a lot of data and computing power, which is available in the enterprise cloud. This rather large model is deployed on the enterprise edge.
3	Depending on the size and specifications of the app, edge-related applications are deployed on the edge server and/or on the programmable devices.
4	A task-specific model, which in this scenario is trained to detect welding flaws, is deployed on the camera, which is watching the output of the robotic welding process. As mentioned, the camera's task is to look for flaws in the welding, such as overlap, undercut, or porous weld.

5	Visual data from step 4 is streamed to the application module controlling the robotic welding machine, which could be a neural network (NN)-based inference engine. If a flaw is detected, corrective action is immediately sent to the robotic weld machine, avoiding an assembly-line stoppage and thus reducing material wastage and costs.
6	Data collected from the vision system is stored on-premises for quick analysis of the current line so that tweaks can be made in the app and/or the model.
7	All data is sent to the enterprise cloud to maintain history and auditability. As described in step 1, this data is used to train/retrain the model before it is redeployed. Other cloud services, such as monitoring and logging, are also provided by the enterprise cloud.

Table 5.2 – Flow of the edge architecture for a manufacturing scenario

The scenario just described dealt with finding welding flaws. The same can be applied to other tasks in a manufacturing process, such as painting and inspecting. The applications deployed on edge devices such as cameras or sensors would differ based on the task being performed at that manufacturing station. Next, we look at a scenario in the retail space.

Retail edge scenario

Large retail stores in rural locations have a different challenge. Network connectivity in such locations isn't very good, so it behooves them to work with telcos to deploy a private 5G network in those areas, which will allow them to have high-speed connectivity. In such a scenario, there would be 5G connectivity to the store and even inside the store. Such a remote location scenario is also a perfect setup where the disconnected edge solution could come into play when there are connectivity glitches.

There are many edge use cases in the retail industry thanks to all those cameras that we see in stores and even some that are hidden. Some of the obvious ones we get to see in our daily lives when we shop are security-related: theft prevention at **point-of-sale** (**POS**) systems, tracking customer movement, product restocking by way of smart shelves, and so on. Among the new ones are what they call "the store of the future" where you get to customize and try the product before buying or immersive shopping, especially in the realm of beauty and apparel using AR/VR technology.

All this is made possible by a couple of things – data and connectivity. Retailers have realized they can get more – and immediate value – from their own store data by analyzing it in real time and acting on it. Imagine sending a discount coupon to the customer while they pick up two or more of the same item. We know that new technologies such as immersive shopping and real-time visual transactions require high-performance computing and low-latency connectivity. Fast connectivity such as 5G gives retailers the bandwidth they need to offer these new technologies. Imagine being able to hold your mobile phone up and the camera shows the store display, highlighting the different merchandise on sale.

Retail store scenario

Whether it is a grocery store or retail merchandise store, edge-/IoT-related solutions are everywhere. Temperature sensors on display freezers, cameras on self-checkout registers, and high-definition shelf monitoring camera systems are some of the devices you see in stores. The four groups of components we described in the previous scenario are also applicable here.

We mentioned different networking options available to enterprises. In this scenario, we describe the option where a grocery store chain is working with a telco to bring 5G networking to its stores. Specifically, the grocery chain has opted for a 5G network slice. Before going any further into the architecture, here's a brief on network slicing.

Network slicing

Network slicing is the ability to create multiple logical "slices" of a single physical core within the 5G network infrastructure using **software-defined networking** (**SDN**). These slices are optimized for specific use cases, types of services, or sets of users. See *Figure 5.5*:

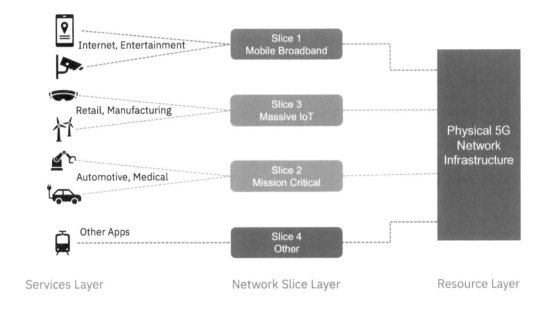

Figure 5.5 – 5G network slicing

SPs also have the option to slice the network in different ways depending on the demands of their customers. *Table 5.2* lists the different slicing types:

Slicing Type	Description
Vertical slicing	This type is industry-focused and designed to serve verticals, such as production optimization, manufacturing, retail, healthcare, and so on. Applications cover public safety, IoT, IPTV, and so on.
Horizontal slicing	This type is more focused on characteristics the slice offers that can support a wide variety of use cases. The slices are created based on characteristics such as bandwidth for downloads and uploads, latency sensitivity, capacity/density sensitivity, symmetric traffic types, and so on.
Static slicing	These are fixed slices that do not change their specifications and are created to cater to specific use cases and capabilities such as M2M and IoT.
Dynamic slicing	Allows SPs to deliver slices in real time and on demand. With this type of network slicing, SPs can quickly provide unique deployments and performance thresholds for individual 5G use cases as required by enterprises or consumers.

Table 5.2 – Network slicing types

Example scenario

In our scenario, a telco will be providing a dedicated slice for all grocery stores in the chain and will be responsible for the management and orchestration of the network connectivity to the stores. It is also possible that the grocery chain might use the regional cloud services of the SP to store data from the stores in the region and use that data to train models. See *Figure 5.6*, which depicts the topology of a solution in a grocery store:

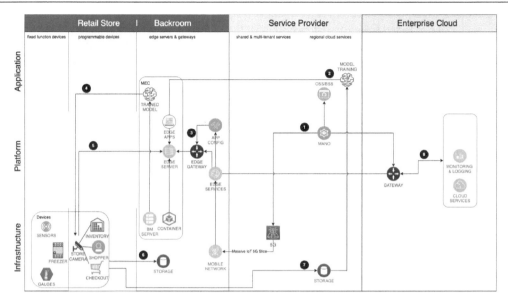

Figure 5.6 – Edge solution architecture in a retail scenario

The architecture flow is explained in *Table 5.3*. The numbers correspond to those depicted in *Figure 5.6*:

No.	Description
1	The network management layer is multi-tenanted and hosted by the SP in the regional cloud that is closer to the customer. MANO plus tasks related to OSS and BSS are handled by the SP from the regional cloud, which is the "managed from" location. A 5G network slice is provided as a secure network for use by all devices in the grocery stores.
2	ML model creation and training requiring a lot of data and computing power are available in the regional network cloud. This model is deployed on the enterprise edge.
3	Depending on the size and specifications of the app, edge-related applications are deployed on the edge server and/or the programmable devices.
4	Task-specific and device-relevant models, which in this scenario are visual inspection models, are deployed onto the cameras that are mounted in various locations in the store. As mentioned, these could be security-related, for theft prevention at POS systems, tracking customer movement, or even for product restocking.
5	Visual data from these cameras is streamed to the application modules that can quickly make inferences and take immediate action. All this is to stop merchandise theft, provide a better customer experience, or provide a personalized shopping touch to in-store shoppers.

6	Data collected from the vision system is stored on-premises for quick analysis of current shopping trends in the store so that the models can be tweaked in real time and made available in the apps.
7	Most of the data is also sent to the regional cloud for maintaining history and auditability and can then be sent to the enterprise cloud to get a corporate view across all stores.
8	Other cloud services, such as monitoring and logging, are provided by the enterprise cloud.

Table 5.3 – Flow of the edge architecture for a retail scenario

We described an edge solution within a grocery store. One can envision replicating this in department stores or home goods stores because the components in play are very similar: inventory shelves, POS systems, backroom, and so on. In the next scenario, we widen the aperture and include some aspects outside the store.

Edge reference architecture

Thus far, most of the discussion has been about edge and 5G components. In this section, an edge scenario is described from an architectural perspective. Cloud and network components, which are "non-edge" components, such as cloud region, **availability zones (AZs)**, load balancers, and other cloud services, are discussed. These components are required to support most edge computing solutions no matter the scenario. *Figure 5.7* shows the cloud components on the right and most of the edge-related components on the left, which would be on-premises:

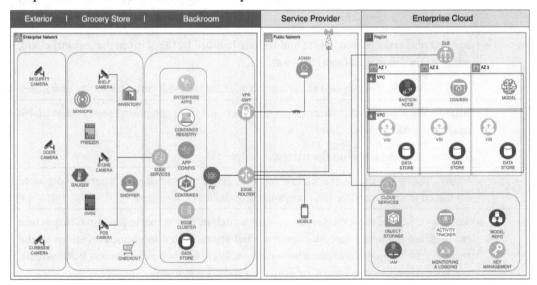

Figure 5.7 – End-to-end edge reference architecture

In this large grocery store scenario, we make an assumption that a CSP will provide the needed 5G network and a hyperscaler will provide all the other IT-related services. *Figure 5.7* shows three distinct areas going from right to left – the cloud, the public network (which is the internet), and the enterprise network.

The cloud

Depending on where the customer (in this example, the grocery store chain) is located, the nearest cloud region is typically chosen to get the best response times when accessing the required cloud services. Every hyperscaler has DCs in multiple regions around the world. Often, these are named US-West or US-East, Europe-North, or Asia-Central.

In our example, if this were a grocery store chain in France, it is quite possible the nearest cloud location could be in Frankfurt in the EU-DE region. Cloud regions have zones often referred to as AZs. Depending on the cloud provider, there are one or more AZs in a region. If available, a production deployment would choose three AZs to support **high availability (HA)**, which would be our recommendation. A global load balancer distributes workloads across the AZs.

The customer may choose to deploy **bare-metal (BM)** servers in the cloud, as they would in their DCs, or opt for a **virtual private cloud (VPC)**, which is more cost-effective. Software and the data required to run are hosted on **virtual server instances (VSIs)** or **virtual private servers (VPSs)**.

Finally, there is a vast array of cloud services to choose from. The most common ones that are used are security- and observability-related, such as **identity and access management (IAM)**, key management, logging, monitoring, container registry, and so on. And last but not least, there is storage – and plenty of it – in the cloud from object store to block store to file store. Depending on the application's needs, the solution architect would determine the type of data store to use.

The network

Networking was covered in detail in the two earlier scenarios. As already mentioned, in this scenario, we simply assume that a CSP will be providing 5G network connectivity to the business.

A secure **virtual private network (VPN)** can be used to connect from the cloud to the enterprise network, or the other option is a high-speed direct connection such as Direct Link or Direct Connect. In either case, the network traffic is encrypted, and it does not traverse the public internet. Access from the internet, if needed, is possible via a secure VPN gateway.

Another route into the store's network would be via the internet for users of the store's mobile application. Known as **buy online, pick up in-store (BOPIS)**, this access method has become very popular now because many users browse and shop for merchandise using the mobile app, place an order online, and then pick up their order in the store or at the curbside.

The edge

As before, it helps to segregate the backroom from the store and the exterior when it comes to the on-premises enterprise network because the IT hardware components are usually in a secured corner in the backroom and we see far-edge and IoT devices dispersed throughout the store, such as freezers, ovens, POS systems, cameras and more. You can even find cameras outside the store in the parking lot or curbside. We alluded to the fact that many of these high-end cameras have some computing power where visual inferencing applications can run.

The edge devices are managed by the edge cluster/node, which is in the backroom. Other related applications such as ML apps or other analytics apps can also be deployed on these edge nodes. Often, these are containerized applications. Depending on how much data the customer wants stored locally, you will also find one or more data stores, albeit in a smaller form factor. There is a firewall protecting these components, and the only access to this on-premises environment is via an edge router.

As you can see, many components make up an edge solution. And depending on the industry and the use case, more variations in edge devices, compute, network, or storage are possible that solution architects must be mindful of.

Edge and distributed cloud computing

In this chapter, detailed industrial and retail architectures have been discussed, but all the solutions depict a single location. Enterprises can duplicate these solutions in their other branches, stores, or locations. This is where we see a new trend that merges edge computing and distributed cloud computing. *Chapter 2* briefly mentioned distributed cloud as one of the new cloud deployment models. We describe it and a corresponding topology in the next scenario.

Distributed cloud computing

In distributed computing, public cloud services are made available in different private physical locations, also known as **satellite locations** or **outposts**. These locations are outside the hyperscaler's facilities and could be on-premises, in another cloud, or even in co-location centers. Distributed cloud computing is not a distributed system.

A **distributed system** is a collection of autonomous computers that work together to create an impression of a single computer. They share resources and operate concurrently but can fail independently.

The scenario

Figure 5.8 shows a managed-from-the-cloud scenario on the right and two remote locations on the left. Plant location *A* in the top left is deployed in a hyperscaler center, and plant location *B* in the bottom left is shown as deployed on-premises. This is important to note because the remote locations can both be on-premises or in the cloud. These cloud locations can be a different hyperscaler than the one managed from the cloud:

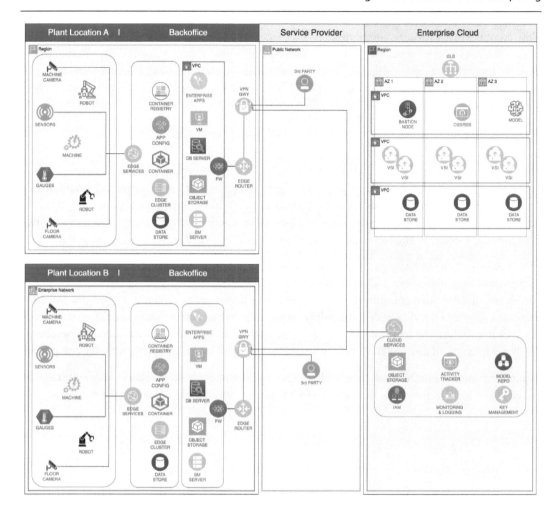

Figure 5.8 – Distributed cloud and edge architecture

In the distributed paradigm, the same cloud services can be extended out to the edge, meaning the same services are available to both plant location *A* and plant location *B*. Imagine an auto manufacturer having multiple locations where different parts are manufactured. They all must adhere to certain specifications while producing different parts that must be assembled together to produce a vehicle. In such a scenario, having access to the same cloud services that control the workflow in the various sub-assemblies would not only maintain consistency across production lines but also provide a single pane of management for the corporate manufacturing department. Plants also have the option to run enterprise applications specific to each location's requirements.

Now, combine that with edge computing practice, wherein each remote location hosts the edge node or clusters from which edge devices can be managed and edge applications can be deployed onto the devices. These devices, as shown in *Figure 5.8*, can be fixed or mobile robots, assembly-line cameras, and other industrial automation devices. We see this trend continuing to evolve as industries find broader use cases.

Summary

The chapter started out with a discussion of IT and OT convergence, which is beneficial to any business in this digital age. Then, we looked at the biggest driver of edge computing – namely, AI; more specifically, AI applications and models that can now be deployed on edge devices. Moving intelligent inferencing and analysis closer to where data is generated provides businesses with not only speed and efficiency but also addresses security and privacy concerns.

In the latter part of the chapter, two end-to-end edge scenarios were described – a manufacturing scenario and a retail scenario. Such scenarios are applicable in almost every industry, but each solution has its own nuances that solution architects should know. For example, if it is a regulated industry scenario, one must worry about data compliance requirements and data security. In a delivery scenario, whether it is delivery by land, air, or sea, one must know and account for disconnected operations. Lastly, we introduced distributed cloud computing and showed how it complements edge computing.

It is imperative that solution architects address data security in every facet of these edge solutions, be it data at rest, data in transit, or data in use. That topic is covered in detail in *Chapter 6*.

Part 3:
Related Considerations and
Concluding Thoughts

The final six chapters in the book apply what was described in Part 1 and formalized in Part 2. These chapters give guidance on when and why to use an approach and when to avoid it. The experience condensed here will give architects the ability to innovate and safely modify the archetypes to fit their specific requirements. The chapters survey many different topics and consider how they apply to edge computing architectures, but these should be taken only as an initial overview, and a springboard to more in-depth research and thinking by the reader, not a comprehensive introduction to the topics.

This part has the following chapters:

- *Chapter 6, Data Has Weight and Inertia*
- *Chapter 7, Automate to Achieve Scale*
- *Chapter 8, Monitoring and Observability*
- *Chapter 9, Connect Judiciously but Thoughtlessly*
- *Chapter 10, Open Source Software Can Benefit You*
- *Chapter 11, Recommendations and Best Practices*

6
Data Has Weight and Inertia

Whether audio, visual, sensory, or telemetry, edge computing is all about data. Whether the data is processed or otherwise transformed at the source where it is generated, stored for later analysis, or used to build models in the future, data is the lifeblood of edge computing. Since data is so valuable, organizations need to store and analyze it before determining relevancy. However, it needs to be done both securely and while actively protecting it in order to meet regulatory compliance regulations. This chapter will discuss considerations about data in its various states. Decisions you make about data will affect *where* data is primarily stored (data at rest) and *how* it is stored. Thus, how it is accessed or transferred (data in motion) becomes a secondary consideration, and tracking how it is used and transformed (data in processing) is critical to having confidence in its trustworthiness.

In this chapter, we will cover the following main topics:

- Data encryption
- Data storage and management
- Using data to build machine learning models
- Connectivity and the data plane

Suggested pre-reading material

- *Security and Privacy by Design or Default (SPbD) principles*: `https://securecontrolsframework.com/domains-principles/`
- *Data Confidence Fabric (Trust Fabric)*: `https://www.lfedge.org/projects/alvarium/`
- *Edge Computing Security: It Starts With Solid Device Identity and Attestation (Medium, Robert Andres)*: `https://medium.com/the-edge-of-things/edge-computing-security-it-starts-with-solid-device-identity-and-attestation-78cace26ed92`

- *Fully Homomorphic Encryption (FHE):* `https://research.ibm.com/blog/fhe-cloud-security-hE4cloud`

- *What is Artificial Intelligence (AI)?:* `https://www.ibm.com/topics/artificial-intelligence`

- *What are Foundation Models?:* `https://research.ibm.com/blog/what-are-foundation-models`

Data encryption

In this section, we will discuss the driving factors for encrypting data, emerging techniques for protecting data while increasing its value, and how to have confidence that data has not been unintentionally or surreptitiously modified. You will learn about protecting data during processing without decrypting. By the end of the section, you should be aware of which techniques work well on the edge.

Motivations for encrypting data

Data is encrypted so that unintended parties cannot read and ultimately use the data. Since the data does not belong to those third parties, nor do they have permission to use it, they should not be able to benefit from the usage of that data – also known as the concept of data ownership. It's about the principle of ownership and the data owner being able to determine to what ends the data and derived value should be put – data sovereignty. Therefore, encryption of data is a method for the data owner to prevent, and to show that they are actively attempting to prevent, unauthorized access to their data and its derived value – to ensure data privacy.

It is similar in intent and purpose to a locked gate and fence around a field. The locked gate is not impervious or impenetrable. Unauthorized visitors could potentially bypass the gate or force it open, for example, but its presence is a clear indication that someone is attempting to prevent access to the field. Circumventing that gate is an act that acknowledges the presence of that barrier and is an overt expression of an intent to bypass that barrier in order to gain entry to the field. Likewise, the presence of encrypted data is an indication that persons without the key are not intended to access the data, and bypassing that encryption is an action showing the intent to use the data despite a lack of permission.

To ensure both that third parties cannot read the data and that they cannot eavesdrop on the data while it is transiting networks or being manipulated in working memory, the data must not only stay encrypted but also be processed in protected memory and be transferred over encrypted and isolated networks – a concept known as data integrity. Additionally, (Perfect) **Forward Secrecy** is a technique that provides additional protections to data in motion by using a new session key to encrypt information each time. This ensures that even if one session's encryption between two parties is compromised, all other sessions between them are still protected. In a perfect world, methods such as those provided by Fully Homomorphic Encryption would be available to process that data and derive value from it without ever decrypting it.

When it comes to edge computing, and especially at the user edge, the expense of encrypting and decrypting data may be higher than at any other location due to less capable hardware driving higher data transmission latencies and slower processing. Additionally, decision-makers may be under the impression that there is no pressing need for *their* data to be encrypted. To help mitigate this misconception, and to ensure that potential vulnerabilities are minimized, it is important that **User Experience** (**UX**) and software development teams be trained in the concepts behind **Security and Privacy by Design** (**SPbD**) and Security and Privacy by Default.

But just encrypting data at rest and data in motion may not be sufficient.

Protecting data without making it difficult to use

Protecting data at rest and in transit can be covered by encrypting the data itself, made more secure by also encrypting transmissions. But this still leaves a potential gap or vulnerability during processing, since the data needs to be decrypted before performing operations on it. But what if the data didn't need to be decrypted to perform computations such as multiplication and addition?

The promise of **Fully Homomorphic Encryption** (**FHE**) is efficient algorithms that can produce encrypted results of calculations that only the owner could subsequently decrypt using the encrypted data as input. This seemingly impossible approach protects data while in processing since the data is never decrypted and the key used to originally encrypt it is not known by the FHE algorithms.

When first developed, FHE tools were needed for financial privacy. They were also thought of as allowing third parties to provide services to perform operations on sensitive and private data without violating confidentiality. However, a new case for FHE has emerged with the practice of training **Machine Learning** (**ML**) models on data. By using FHE, which supports floating point math operations, models can be trained on data that cannot be directly read, and that only the data owner could then subsequently decrypt and use.

A drawback to the use of FHE, especially on the edge, is the amount of processing required, and the amount of time it may take to process. This means that using FHE for near real-time calculations will likely require cloud-based resources. But if the use case isn't as time-critical, edge computing may be sufficient for these techniques.

So, making data difficult, if not impossible, for an untrusted party to read and use is a great start. But how do you know whether the data has been manipulated by others?

Ensuring that data modifications are noticeable

Protecting data is not just about preventing others from reading and using the data. It's also about knowing where the data came from (provenance), whether it has been modified since it was generated, by whom, and whether the parties in the chain of custody can be trusted (lineage). One mechanism to collect and report on all that metadata is a **Data Confidence Fabric** (**DCF**).

DCFs can generate data confidence scoring values to indicate how likely it is that a piece of data came from the indicated origin, and assurance about which subsequent systems and applications it has traversed, thus giving a degree of certainty that the documented chain of ownership has been correctly captured. DCFs can also indicate the likelihood of whether and when data has been modified, based on a collected history of annotations written to immutable storage by trust insertion technologies and thus associating the history of the data record with the record itself.

Consequently, data with a high confidence score is likely to be trustworthy, and data with lower scores is either known to be untrustworthy or of unknown provenance and lineage. In any event, only data with high scores is unlikely to have been manipulated and is thus objectively trustworthy. The benefits of using a DCF include being able to trust data sourced from a third party, and knowing how data has traveled, along with any modifications along that journey.

Since data from sensors, actuators, and other IoT sources are typically generated at the edge, this is the primary location to begin implementing a DCF-based solution. To do so, base your planning on four considerations:

- Choose a trusted DCF solution (such as Project Alvarium, `https://alvarium.org/`) used by organizations in the same type of business, vertical, or industry.

- Ensure the IoT devices that you use can support a hardware-based root of trust or similar technology that definitively identifies the device. Build in a device attestation strategy, utilizing a chain of certificates to confirm both the integrity and trustworthiness of every device.

- Identify all locations where you need to integrate trust insertion technologies.

- Deploy trust insertion only in configurations with reliable, stable, and constant network connectivity to the DCF.

A positive consequence of using DCFs is that compliance with privacy standards becomes much easier due to the proof it provides of what has and has not been done to the data. In the next section, we will cover solutions to manage your data.

Data storage and management

In this section, we cover data storage considerations, viable alternatives to data retention, and data catalogs/governance/policy enforcement in edge computing. You will learn about considerations to weigh when implementing data management solutions. By the end of the section, you should be able to articulate what data management processes you will follow and what tools you plan to use to enforce the processes and policies.

Strategies for defining and enforcing data policies

Over the last several years, we've seen governments around the world propose and implement legislation aimed at protecting private data, beginning with the EU's **General Data Privacy Regulation (GDPR)**. This type of legislation has encouraged organizations to be more intentional about what data they collect, how they store, use, and share it, and for how long and where it is retained.

For organizations to comply with these privacy regulations, there are three foundational solution components that should be used. These include a data catalog, data policy sets comprised of rules, and data policy enforcement mechanisms to ensure that those rules are followed without exception. Let's explore each one of these to understand the scope of responsibility of each of these data management solutions, and briefly discuss how edge computing may affect deployment considerations.

Data catalogs are solutions that collect descriptions of collected data, data types, sources, data purposes, collection timestamps, access rules, storage formats, and other metadata related to answering the questions "What data is being collected, from whom, and why"? There are at least three considerations that will affect what data catalog solutions you choose to employ and where they should be deployed:

- **Consideration 1**: These catalogs are typically accessed by data scientists and others doing research, analysis, and business intelligence reporting and summarizing, which means that they are typically centrally located

- **Consideration 2**: They may also be accessed by automated systems querying and enforcing data policies, which means that they should be located near data storage, especially if connectivity is not always available

- **Consideration 3**: In the case of distributed data storage strategies where the data is kept as close to the source as practical, this implies that a description of that data should accompany the storage or querying capability

Data policy sets and rules are a way of encoding an institution's official procedures for data access, usage, retention, and movement in a machine-readable format so they can then be enforced. The policy sets and rules also serve as proof of intent that the organization knows data should be protected and is actively striving to do so.

These data policy rulesets, like the catalog, need to be centrally located and accessed but also need to be available in offline scenarios. For this reason, we recommend a central ruleset storage location with caching or distribution to edge locations. Or, alternatively, using a solution that generates rules as code and distributing the resulting application to edge locations.

To have a complete data governance solution, you not only need to know what the data is, its provenance and lineage, and how it should be used, but you also must enforce those rulesets. This requires that data reads, writes, and deletes must be mediated by logic that understands the complete context of the transaction: who is requesting it, for what purpose, in what geographic location, with what consuming application, and for what (data) purpose. That logic must understand the data, its metadata, the request context, and applicable data policy rulesets.

In light of the above discussion of data governance rules, the resulting policies constitute the maximum length of time that personal or private data may be kept. The minimums are more flexible and can be based on the cost of data retention, the amount of available storage, and other practical considerations. An exception to those bounds may be data that your organization is legally required to retain.

With the restrictions that privacy legislation requires come limitations on how the data can be used. However, there are some techniques available that would provide similar outcomes to using personal data without violating the data subject's privacy. Those data usage options will be discussed next.

Usage options ranging from real to synthetic data

Many years ago, architects and developers working at a top website were reviewing the web server infrastructure access logs to determine what statistics and site/section/page usage data to surface. Product managers would need to learn how visitors interacted with the site, how long they lingered on various pages and sections, and what pages they likely visited accidentally, or were navigational dead-ends. Technical staff would need to see which pages were generating errors for visitors, and which were too large or taking too long to load. Information architects and SEO staff would evaluate the URLs, seeing how the site was indexed and read by machines (site crawlers, indexing routines, and screen readers), and ensuring that all content was translated equally into all supported languages.

Every one of those persons needed insights from the log files, but some of the information contained therein was considered personal data and could reasonably be used to positively identify a specific person (which would violate their expectations of privacy). Except for the singular case of resolving technical support issues, none of the staff needed access to information classified as Restricted Data (IP address, location data, date and time of request, authentication, usernames, and even some referral information). So the challenge for the architects was determining the most efficient method of surfacing the required information without revealing the sensitive data. Here are some heuristics we developed to ensure that we didn't inadvertently break any rules, violate user privacy, or even display or use information that we shouldn't.

The first and most obvious option is not to store or otherwise persist any data if it is not going to be used or *should not* be used. Next would be retaining data that can be stored, but should not be viewable by *all* persons with access. Third would be masking any sensitive information when displaying records to those authorized to view portions of the data. Fourth would be preventing access to the data by unauthorized parties. And fifth would be removing the data when its retention period had expired or the data subject had requested its removal. Let's examine each of these rules of thumb in turn:

- Keep only the data you need. The next topic to be covered in this chapter section will be data retention strategies for the edge. This topic will address how to categorize your data and then determine rules for each category.

- Restrict access to your data. This requires data policies and enforcement solutions to be implemented as discussed in the preceding *Data storage and management* section.

- Data access rules should be granular. The solutions that display data should have filtering solutions in place that know each viewer and what data they are or are not authorized to view. The presentation of sensitive data should then be blocked or masked when it should not be viewed in that context.

- Actively prevent some data access. This may mean having your data access solution return an error message when access should be prevented, or blocking access at a higher level in the application stack.

- Prune your data. Don't assume that data is immutable, given that some records will need to be removed at a time short of the data retention limit. Always ensure that records marked for removal can either be removed in an acceptable amount of time or that they can be dereferenced and not otherwise retrieved.

However, there are times when a change in the way you use your data can remove the complexity the preceding rules of thumb require. If you were able to modify the data that you collect *before* using and storing it so that all restricted data is replaced with equivalent fictional data that would give statistically equivalent results *in the aggregate*, then many data access and restriction rules could potentially be relaxed. This would also result in your data management overhead being proportionately reduced. This type of replacement data is termed synthetic data.

Synthetic data can be used to replace usage data on the whole but not individual personal or account records. It may also have the potential to reduce the overall *amount* of data that needs to be retained. However, you will still need to have active data retention processes and governance in place for your data as a whole. Let's look at those considerations now.

Rules of thumb for retaining data, or not

A connected car expert recently said that when roughly half of the billion cars on the road today are comprised of connected cars, they will generate 30 zettabytes of data a year. How much of that data is analyzed, or even needed?

You can classify data in many ways, depending on your vocation, industry, or practices. In data science, data is classified based on what is known about it:

- **Context-based**: When aspects of its creation are known and affect the data

- **Content-based**: When the contents of the data affect the category it is assigned to

- **User-based**: When a human labeling the data determines its usage

Data comes in two forms: structured and unstructured. Structured data is organized to fit a data schema or model, and unstructured data is not. Management of data in storage systems categorizes data by its retention needs: short-term data, long-term data, and useless data. Compliance and security professionals also label (classify) data as one of the following five types: restricted, confidential, internal-only, private, and public.

Unlike data science classification, data on the regional and user edge falls into one of two types: system data and user data. System, or operational, data can be used to configure and operate architectural elements. System data is structured and persisted as needed. User, or generated, data is created or captured by edge devices. User data can be structured (temperature readings) or unstructured (acoustic monitoring). See *Figure 6.1* for strategies on deciding how to manage edge data.

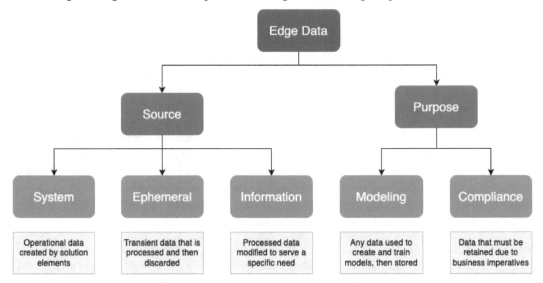

Figure 6.1 - Thinking about data retention at the edge by data origin and usage

Based on the preceding chart, if data is not used to configure or operate solutions, is not processed for a business intelligence purpose, and is not required to be retained, then you might not need to store the data after initial processing is complete.

Next, let's discuss how edge data can be used for model generation and training, and strategies for model-based inferencing on the user and regional edges.

Using data to build machine learning (ML) models

In this section, you will read about techniques for efficient (re)training, inferencing, deployment, and customizing ML models. We will also discuss what has prevented high levels of demand from being met, and what is being done to resolve that.

Before we dive into the topic, it's appropriate to briefly review **Artificial Intelligence** (**AI**) and what distinguishes it from ML and **Deep Learning** (**DL**). IBM describes AI as *"leverage[ing] computers and machines to mimic the problem-solving and decision-making capabilities of the human mind."* See *"What is Artificial Intelligence (AI)?"* in the *Suggested pre-reading material* section at the beginning of the chapter for a deeper explanation and some background history. ML is a branch of AI and a component of the field of data science that uses data and algorithms to imitate the way we believe human brains acquire knowledge. ML typically uses structured or labeled data and human intervention (supervised learning) to learn and make predictions (infer a result). DL consumes large amounts of unstructured data and may not need supervised learning to create useful models. Both ML and DL models typically cover a single domain of knowledge and are thus highly specific to one type of task.

The promise of foundation models

Three factors that delay or prevent widespread adoption of ML-powered automation include long training times and the cost, steep learning curves and limited expert availability, and big resource requirements using expensive **Graphical Processing Unit (GPU)** hardware for inferencing using the models. Every advance made that addresses those factors has the potential to make these tools less expensive to operate and thus more profitable to use, enabling employees to be more productive by accomplishing more tasks with greater accuracy in less time.

Foundation models, unlike ML and DL models, are trained on very large sets of data, which are usually unlabeled. The resulting models can then be fine-tuned for many different (but related) purposes, unlike single-purpose ML and DL models. This can make foundation models more efficient and quicker to initially build, but also to repurpose for other tasks.

The promise is that instead of groups of humans curating large amounts of source data and then spending weeks or longer training ML or DL models just to solve a specific problem, an enterprise can use fewer people to train a single foundation model and then fine-tune it to solve many problems. To shorten the process even further, an organization could start with an existing foundation model from a trusted source and only add the needed fine-tuning for its specific purpose. Thus, leveraging foundation models requires fewer persons and can reduce the time to value for a business from weeks to days.

The trade-off with foundation models is that they are so large that they need to be run in a cloud environment or large data center. Conversely, some ML models can be optimized to run on single machines or even highly constrained devices. Therefore, ML models could be deployable to the user edge, while DL models might be deployable to the service provider edge.

Additionally, using federated learning techniques allows multiple data sources (such as distributed data, for example) to be used to train a single deep learning model. This horizontal federated learning approach works by having each data source trained on its local data using a single shared model, and then sending the results back to the original model source (usually in the cloud). This can be more efficient and faster than sending the data to the source for training.

How small and efficient can we make models?

While there is plenty of demand for the usage of ML to perform repetitive tasks and surface insights as close to where the data originates as possible, there are several factors preventing this. First is the **availability** of GPUs and other accelerators. Second is the **cost** of purchasing and operating that hardware. And third is the lack of general-purpose tools that will **customize** and train the ML models as close to where they are needed as is practical. Fortunately, teams are actively working to solve all of these challenges.

At the time of writing this chapter, a new article was just posted showing how MIT, IBM, and researchers in China just created a new technique named EfficientViT for semantic segmentation (object detection) that improves performance over traditional approaches nine-fold. They anticipate that this innovation will allow near real-time object detection *locally* with improved accuracy on constrained edge devices. Solutions like this one will affect both cost and availability at the edge by more efficiently utilizing existing hardware.

Just this year, it has become common to see single-purpose ML models no larger than a few hundred **megabytes** (**MBs**) in size created to run on inexpensive microcontrollers, which are not typically thought of as capable of running these workloads. Factories are now using inexpensive consumer-grade mobile phones, instead of specialized hardware, to run visual inspection tasks using ML models less than a **gigabyte** (**GB**) in size and optimized for the onboard GPU.

Customizing existing models for each deployment

When determining the optimum parameters to consider when evaluating a model, you should consider the factors of size (as it impacts both storage and deployment speed), (re)training cost, operating cost, and the inference speed of the model when matching to the desired hardware it will run on. Your KPIs should be used to assign the appropriate weights to each category. For example, if your primary concern is operating cost and the speed of inferencing isn't critical, then it's acceptable to weigh operating efficiency much higher than performance.

Just as important are the types of models that the GPU or other accelerators support. If there is any incompatibility, the inferencing environment will likely fall back to using the CPU, which will incur a significant performance penalty. Even slight differences in how a model was created, including quantizing methods, could affect the performance, so careful attention to model creation parameters should be prioritized. Given the heterogeneous nature of hardware on the edge, it is likely that there will be incompatibilities.

Thirdly, choose a model deployment solution that can deliver model assets to the consuming edge node. This will both guarantee confirmation of artifact delivery to the endpoint and also allow the deployment solution to communicate attributes of the edge node including GPU type, available storage space, and computing power to the delivery pipeline so that accurate placement decisions can be made. This type of model deployment solution is a good example of a general-purpose platform, which is our next topic.

Using general-purpose platforms rather than single-purpose applications

When decision-makers set out to use their data to build ML models (especially for edge-based operations), they are usually being tactical and attempting to either solve a single problem or a class of related problems. Starting the evaluation process with constraints like these limits the potential range of solutions being considered to a set of competing single-purpose applications. In fact, considering an application to solve the particular problem at hand is the typical knee-jerk reaction. Instead, we'd like to propose an alternative course of action.

On a recent community call discussing the Open Retail Reference Architecture (ORRA), I heard an insight delivered in an off-hand manner that got my attention. Kristen Call, senior industry advisor at Intel Corporation, while discussing the value of edge-based platforms, said: "Don't buy a purpose-built solution. Your data *is* the solution, build on it." Her point was that it is easy to find a single tool that solves a particular problem, but that is the end of the value that it provides. Each application installed consumes finite resources on edge computing nodes (devices and clusters) and must be carefully considered. A question each architect should ask is: "Does this tool provide value for more than just this one solution"?

Solutions should not be siloed, and potential derived insights should not be lost. But if a store were running a general-purpose edge computing platform that enabled sensor fusion, it could export insights and generate business rules dynamically in a way that provides value to both the store and the shopper in a manner that no single application could.

For example, if on one trip to your grocery store, you were to purchase three items – steak, corn, and beer – the platform could store that information and note that those three items were purchased together by a shopper. One insight could be that they might be preparing to cook out. Another could be recommendations that in similar situations, other shoppers also purchased napkins, single-use tableware, condiments, tablecloths, and dinner candles. A third would be matching to current store specials and promoting those related items. If the shopper had the store application installed on their phone, it could push those recommendations to the shopper when they make a shopping list or when they enter the store or approach the checkout.

The point of the preceding scenario is that none of those would be possible if the purchase data were stored in a single application. Surfacing of the data insights would not be possible without a general-purpose platform. Using the insights to create solutions is a lot simpler with the tools a platform provides when compared to the cost and maintenance of integrating single-purpose solutions – if their interfaces even enable that. Ultimately, a platform that enables innovation, especially if it provides a low-code or no-code interface, provides a flexible foundation while at the same time promoting efficient use of edge computing resources on-premises.

Since we've now mooted that your data is the solution, let's move on to discussing how to optimally access that data while minimizing its movement.

Connectivity and the data plane

In this section, we cover issues related to data at rest and in motion, specifically from the perspective of edge computing, data virtualization and the edge, and transparent progressive failover starting at the edge and moving cloudward. You will learn about various options available to edge computing architectures that will assist in automating data management, placement, and migration capabilities.

Optimizing data availability without connectivity

Part and parcel of manipulating and storing data is the movement of data, which necessarily includes connectivity. But what if that connectivity is not available, is intermittent, or is slow with low throughput and high latency? How can you ensure that all local data is available to all services and applications that can access it even while remote data is not?

One technique to consider is using a data virtualization solution that can access local data in any format and allow SQL-like querying of structured and unstructured data. While that data could be persisted in an object store, it does not have to be. There are several solutions available that implement data virtualization and querying functionality like this.

Another technique would be to ensure that all functionality is available without an internet connection. In *Chapter 3*'s *Disconnected operation* section, we touched on the AgriRegio Projekt's "offline-first principle." Let's examine that in more detail and look at the impact on and considerations for data collection and transfer as a best practice approach. See *Figure 6.2* for an overview of the farm deployment.

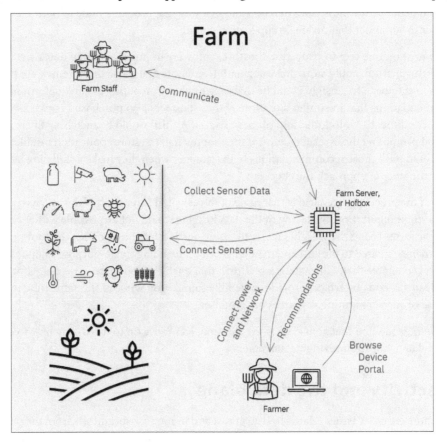

Figure 6.2 - How the farm box (Hofbox) manages data without the internet

On the typical small farm under consideration (less than five acres on average), there will be sensors deployed to measure moisture, sunlight, and water depth in a stream, capture images, and so on. These sensors will be placed semi-permanently (moved fewer than 13 times a year), permanently, or temporarily. They collect data measurements at rates ranging from once a minute to once a day. These sensors should be able to store or buffer that data for a limited amount of time – usually, not more than a week's worth of data before potential data loss occurs.

The data that is captured is the property of the farm owner and should be controlled by the owner. The farm owner's dwelling would contain an edge gateway server named the Hofbox that would be the central storage, processing, and reporting location for all collected data. We anticipate that data will be transferred from the sensors to the Hofbox in one of three manners: direct transmission from sensors to server by Wi-Fi or LoRa, indirect transmission by network mesh (Wi-Fi, LoRa, Bluetooth), or manual transfer by connecting a mobile device to the sensor with USB to retrieve the data and then subsequently connecting the mobile to the server with Wi-Fi. Of note in the preceding scenarios is that no internet connection of any kind is needed to collect and transmit the data.

The data management is provided by containerized applications running on the farm server, which may include object recognition and other visual analytics aided by ML models. An internet connection would only be needed to transmit collected data to a regional hub if the farmer opted in, to install new applications, and to update existing applications and re-trained models. That internet connection would only need to be active during the transmission period.

This approach is possible when following edge-native architectural principles, as discussed in *Chapter 1*. For a more detailed discussion of thriving in situations with ambiguous connectivity, see *Chapter 9*.

Aggregating data versus keeping it distributed

When IoT devices first began to be connected to the internet, cloud- and data center-based central aggregation and processing of the data was best practice. This was because the resulting solution could be highly available and scalable, and could be relatively inexpensive to operate. At the time, there was no capability for any reasonable processing to happen outside of the cloud or regional data centers, and cloud-native development was still in its infancy.

Now, almost a decade since that time, two advancements have completely altered the solution landscape. The first change is the ability to generate insights from data streams in stages, at the source and then, optionally, regionally before consuming the results and/or aggregating in the cloud (if needed). The second change is the ability to virtualize and thus query the data where it is generated without transferring to, or aggregating the data at, a central location. This ability to extract value and insights directly from the data source simplifies solutions, delivers results faster, and reduces expenses dramatically.

This edge computing data virtualization revolution began with the GaianDB open source project. Since then, it has seen several iterations and subsequent expansions and improvements. Other organizations have combined that approach with additive innovations such as ad hoc P2P network underlays and embedded device support.

We are now at the point where IoT routers and IoT hubs (see *Chapter 3* for a detailed discussion on these elements) are now largely obsolete as data on fixed-function devices can be injected directly into a data virtualization solution at the source and immediately queried from any edge or cloud node. This is a drastic simplification over the former process of legacy protocol support, data ingestion into an IoT platform, data transformation, message queueing, transport, and finally, importing into a database to be queried. And yet, data virtualization has yet to be widely adopted, and there are few enterprise-grade solutions available that stretch from the cloud to the edge. We expect a sea change in this regard within the next few years as architects recommend, and CXOs embrace, this approach to upgrade, modernize, and automate existing solutions.

One other reason not to keep data distributed in the past was the need to aggregate data in a single location for training machine learning models. Using federated learning techniques to incrementally and independently train models has now eliminated another objection to keeping data distributed.

Migrating data files automatically

As stated earlier in the chapter, when looking for solutions, prefer a general-purpose platform or tool over a single-purpose application (off-the-shelf or homegrown) since it will provide more flexibility with less maintenance. And if that general solution adheres to open or industry standards, so much the better. We've covered querying and streaming data records, both locally and remotely. Now it's time to turn our attention to data files.

A typical challenge when accessing files locally on edge devices is determining when and how to archive the files, where to put them when archiving so that it does not take too long to retrieve them nor incur excessive or unbudgeted costs in doing so, and how to access them later without knowing deterministically where to look for them. Let's examine those issues one at a time.

Automatically archiving files on a schedule when they pass a certain age threshold since creation, or when the filesystem volume passes a pre-specified percentage full, is a technique typically used. This approach can work when files are added in a predictable manner, provided that the process doesn't fail silently. However, it is not adequate when new files are added between scheduled times. Most tools also do not intercept attempted writes and force a cleanup/archiving routine while pausing the write until the cleanup operation is complete. Conventional methods completely fail if the file is larger than the target storage volume.

Determining where to put the files is an issue when you have multiple potential destinations, such as hot, warm, and cold storage options, regional storage options, and multiple cloud vendors with variable pricing.

Knowing where files are currently located would require following a specified formula, using a global lookup mechanism, or trying each location sequentially while falling back when not found. Each one of these options can incur a latency penalty and require complex configuration and maintenance.

Thus, the best practice approach would be to use a general-purpose edge-native unified storage solution that stores files locally, regionally, and globally (example: Nexoedge `https://lfedge.org/projects/nexoedge/`). This solution would need to function as a proxy on the edge nodes and allow local file operations to act on the files no matter where they are currently stored. The solution would need to move files in the background as they are accessed more or less frequently, and as space, connectivity, and costs allow.

Summary

In this chapter, we covered the states of data at rest, data in motion, and data in processing. You have learned about how, when, and why to encrypt data, including the ability to perform operations on the data without decrypting it using fully homomorphic encryption. You were introduced to the idea of data trustworthiness using a data confidence fabric, which can be implemented on the least powerful machines on the user edge where data is born.

You learned about data storage and management approaches, including data governance, policies, and enforcement, as well as ways to simplify management and lower costs with synthetic data. You were also introduced to a way of thinking about data retention on the edge that will lead to simplified decisions.

We also covered how to optimize machine learning models for the edge. This could include using foundation models to simplify and speed up training. And we touched on model federation. We discussed the benefit of general-purpose platforms over single-purpose applications.

Then, we talked about how connectivity affects data collection and usage. We gave an example of how to use edge-native architecture principles to ensure constant access to data by decision-makers. We showed how data does not need to be aggregated northward but can be queried as needed while keeping it distributed. We also touched on ways to migrate data and files automatically.

In the next chapter, we'll discuss how to efficiently put these lessons into practice by automating (almost) everything.

7

Automate to Achieve Scale

Deploying applications and models to hundreds and thousands of edge devices and edge clusters/ nodes, then monitoring and managing all these things, is a challenge and not for the faint of heart. With the proliferation of these heterogeneous edge devices and the services required in an edge solution, it is almost impossible to manually deploy applications on these devices and manage them at scale, especially when it comes to networking components. The more prudent approach would be to introduce automation. In fact, it is an absolute necessity.

From monitoring the devices to updating the applications and models running on those devices, the goal of automation is to allow enterprises to build capabilities that can act and react with the solution components in a more secure and trusted manner with minimal human interaction. The other facet of automation is the ability to scale. An automated process should work for hundreds and thousands of devices whether it is to configure things or to roll things back. Like the digital journey or the AI journey, automation in the deployment of edge computing components is now trending more toward automation facilitated by open source communities such as LF Edge.

This chapter dives into areas where automation can help speed up deployment tasks and help **information technology** (**IT**) and **operations team** (**OT**) staff. The following topics are covered in this chapter:

- Automating service delivery
- Attaining scalability with automation
- Remote operational security
- Automation with **artificial intelligence** (**AI**)

Whether it is to manage edge devices more efficiently, apply configurations more consistently across varied and heterogeneous infrastructure, or distribute updates or patches, the goal of automation is to be able to do all of this automatically and flawlessly.

Most of the topics discussed thus far have had to do with the architecture, configuration, and setup of an edge computing topology or solution, which fall into the category of day 1 tasks. This chapter on automation addresses not only day 1 operations but also day 2 tasks, which have more to do with maintaining a system. Solution architects must always keep day 2 operations in mind when architecting a solution because a well-architected solution ensures a healthy system, which is best achieved with deployment automation.

Automating service delivery

The goal of service delivery is to reduce the number of steps required to deliver a service. This is true in IT as well as in edge computing. Whether it is a simple application or a **machine learning** (**ML**) model to be deployed on edge devices quickly and securely, automating those steps is what teams strive for. Doing so helps eliminate configuration errors and scale such solutions.

Physical installation of devices is not something that the OT can automate, but the configuration of the devices and deployment of applications that run on those devices can be automated. If a large bank that has over 10,000 ATMs across the country wants to apply an update to its ATMs, it cannot afford to send personnel to every ATM. Rather, the update is done remotely either through command-line scripts or a DevOps toolchain. Another good example is damage detection sensors on wind turbine blades monitored by edge nodes located on top of the wind turbines.

DevOps

Collaboration between **development** (**Dev**) and **operations** (**Ops**) has given us a set of processes known as **DevOps**, which allows for a pipeline to develop, test, deploy, and monitor code in a continuous manner. This is done with a set of open source tools, such as Ansible and Eclipse IDE, that work together in the form of a toolchain.

> **EdgeOps**
>
> Not all DevOps features are applicable to edge computing, especially continuous delivery, because as we know, some devices operate in disconnected mode. EdgeOps is a new paradigm that addresses edge computing-specific aspects, which can vary and be less predictable compared to cloud environments due to the heterogeneous nature of the edge hardware. This article from the Eclipse Foundation explains the EdgeOps project: `https://www.eclipse.org/community/eclipse_newsletter/2021/february/2.php`.

Infrastructure as code

Infrastructure as code (**IaC**) uses the DevOps methodology to describe the layout of IT infrastructure and provides the ability to provision and manage resources. These resources include compute, storage, and network. They can be in the cloud, in a data center, or even at the edge.

There are many automation frameworks that enterprises can choose from, including Ansible, Chef, Puppet, and Terraform. There are pros and cons to each of these frameworks.

Enterprises either end up using what their developers are comfortable with or rely on the recommendation of their cloud provider. Ansible and Terraform are probably the two top automation frameworks (see the reviews on `https://www.techrepublic.com`). While both help with automating provisioning and deployment tasks, and both are open source and cloud agnostic, there are subtle differences. See *Table 7.1* for the differences:

Terraform	Ansible
An IaC software tool that is used to automate building, provisioning, and managing IT resources	A suite of command-line software tools that are used as IaC to automate application deployment and configuration management tasks in IT
Written in the Go language	Written in the Python language
Uses a declarative approach	Uses both declarative and procedural approach

Table 7.1: Differences between Terraform and Ansible

Chapter 9 provides more detail about the declarative and procedural styles of coding.

> **GitOps**
>
> GitOps extends IaC by including Git as the single source of truth where the infrastructure and application deployment manifest files are stored. All changes are initiated from Git.

Extending automation to the edge

The challenge has been automating the proverbial last mile when it comes to edge computing. The reason for that is the small footprint of far edge devices. Deploying infrastructure to and at the edge is best accomplished using a DevOps toolchain. DevOps toolchain diagrams are usually shown as a sideways figure 8 loop and encompass IT and OT tasks working seamlessly.

A DevOps pipeline, on the other hand, is a set of agreed-upon processes and related tools that allow developers to do their development tasks and collaborate with operations to deploy the coded applications. *Figure 7.1* shows a pipeline with tools that help in building, testing, and deploying an edge server.

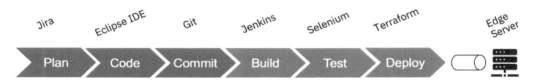

Figure 7.1 - DevOps pipeline to deploy edge infrastructure

With this diagram, we simply wanted to get the point across that the steps to configure an edge server/cluster are rather straightforward. The tools shown are example open source tools.

When it comes to deploying applications to edge servers/clusters and far-edge devices, a similar set of tools could be used but there would be two pipelines. The first pipeline would deploy the application to the edge server or cluster, and a second pipeline would be used to deploy container-based applications on the far edge devices. See *Figure 7.2*.

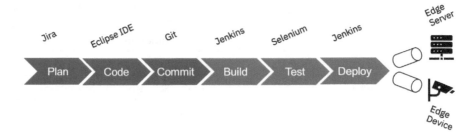

Figure 7.2 - DevOps pipeline to deploy an edge application

We talked about deploying edge infrastructure and applications on edge devices. What about developing edge applications? Let's take a brief look at Open Horizon. *Chapter 10* describes everything you need to know about Open Horizon.

Open Horizon, which is a project from the `Linux Foundation` (`https://www.lfedge.org/projects/openhorizon/`), is an open source platform for the development and autonomous management of software applications that are deployed on edge devices or nodes. Information about DevOps support in Open Horizon can be found at `https://github.com/open-horizon/devops`.

Developing edge applications

The fun thing about edge computing is that anyone can create a simple application and deploy it to an edge device such as Raspberry Pi, a robot, a drone, or a Jetson Nano camera. Obviously, creating and maintaining applications that perform visual analytics or data inferencing requires expertise in several different fields of software development. The following code snippet is a very simple Hello World service that outputs **Hello from Packt** every five seconds. Such a simple edge service is typically used to test and confirm that an edge device is working properly:

```sh
#!/bin/sh
# Simple edge service
while true; do
    echo "HZN_DEVICE_ID says: Hello from Packt!"
    sleep 5
done
```

The service also outputs the device ID, which in a real-world use case is an easy way to identify the device. If you notice closely, it is an Open Horizon environment variable, namely `HZN_DEVICE_ID`. You could choose not to have it and make the program even more simple. If you want to get all the supporting code that deploys the service, you can find it on the Open Horizon GitHub repository (`https://github.com/open-horizon/examples/blob/master/edge/services/helloworld/CreateService.md`).

Scalability with automation

We often hear the term **automation at scale**, which really means using data analytics and ML tools to help with automation across an organization. From an edge computing perspective, it would translate to having automation as we move from right to left—from the cloud to the network to the enterprise all the way to the far edge devices.

Now imagine, if that trivial program shown previously was to be deployed on hundreds of cameras in a large automotive manufacturing plant, the IT department would use a configuration and management software tool to do that. The biggest benefit of automation is being able to scale and, very importantly, roll back if every device is not updated. No matter the number of devices, one or more DevOps pipelines would help with that task. Once tested, the same deployment task can be repeated many times without the concern of introducing any human errors.

Prepping an edge device

We have talked a lot about edge devices and their variances in form, size, and use. But what does it take to onboard an edge device such as a camera or a robot? The edge device/node owner takes on that responsibility and performs five tasks, as shown in *Figure 7.3*.

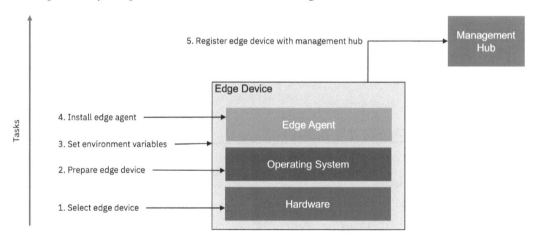

Figure 7.3 - Steps to prep an edge device

The high-level tasks are as follows:

1. Select the appropriate device, making sure the type of hardware is supported by the proposed edge solution.

2. Prep the device by installing the minimal operating system.

3. Set various environment variables.

4. Install an agent so that it can be registered with an edge management hub.

5. Register the edge device with an edge management hub in order to run edge services.

Once the edge device is registered, the management hub can monitor it and the device can also be added as an endpoint in a DevOps toolchain so that applications can be deployed to it.

The tasks shown previously must be done for each edge device that needs to be part of the edge solution. Zero-touch provisioning solutions make it possible to automate the initial imaging and configuration of new nodes. The zero-touch paradigm is described in *Chapter 9*. From a scalability perspective, and even from the perspective of IoT devices that do not have compute and storage, there is another option, which is to prep an edge cluster that is connected to such IoT devices. The steps are very similar.

Prepping an edge cluster

A solution architect must be aware of when using edge clusters makes sense. **Edge clusters** are usually container-based clusters and are used either in colocation scenarios or in situations when more scalability and computing capability are needed to support many edge devices. The tasks are shown in *Figure 7.4*.

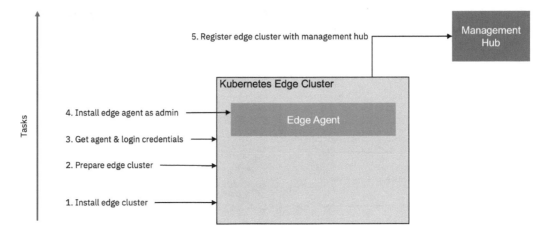

Figure 7.4 - Steps to prep an edge cluster

The OT gets involved when setting up an edge cluster. As before, after the edge cluster is registered, the management hub can monitor it and it can be added as an endpoint in a DevOps toolchain so that applications can be deployed to it.

Operational security

As your IT team/OT manages day 1 provisioning and deployment tasks based on the architecture and plans defined during day 0, let's address operational security issues from both a planning and process perspective, with emphasis on aspects that may be unique to edge computing. In this section, we'll discuss limiting access in all layers of the architecture, how that applies to automation, and an example based on the concept of the Tactical Edge. As you read through this section, consider creating a custom checklist containing the items and considerations that apply to your specific architecture deployment scenario and then review it with the staff that will be working on the deployment.

Limiting physical access

When it comes to regional deployments at the service provider edge, most access to equipment is managed by the facility staff and infrastructure. But when it comes to field deployments at the user edge, there can be little to no consistency or standardization. Some servers may be in racks, mounted in a room, or out in the open. Other edge devices may be wall mounted or sitting on a shelf or desk. Ensure that devices are in a locked room or otherwise out of sight and arrange for local staff to inspect the devices on a regular, scheduled basis. If practical, see whether automated visual monitoring of high-value hardware can be added to your architecture as a requirement.

Likewise, consider hardware specifications that include cases that limit physical access to device inputs, such as connectors, plugs, and slots, and that allow physical connections to be locked in place. If an unauthorized person cannot plug an external device into your hardware after it has been deployed, that is one less way to exploit your solutions. Lastly, ensure the hardware cannot be booted from an externally mounted storage device, and that you use trusted boot technology.

Limiting connectivity

When deploying devices in the field, it is important to consider the ways in which a device can communicate, enumerating the allowed methods from that list, and then disabling all other methods. It may not be enough to disable functionality in the software, so consider physically altering the hardware to prevent the use of that function. Likewise, see whether you can determine the allowed hosts that the device may communicate with, and ensure that no other host is allowed to communicate.

If practical, disable all inbound communications and only allow the device to initiate outbound communications. The rule of thumb is the same as the standard zero-trust approach: deny all, then allow some as required. Any automation tools and configurations you use should implement this pattern. Ensure that your architectures and resulting requirements communicate this clearly and firmly, and that tests verify that it has been implemented for all frequencies, transports, protocols, and ports. Consider using device management solutions that track and automate the collection and control of this information and functionality, and only trust solutions that provide source code to allow independent verification.

Trusted hardware and provisioning

Additionally, solution architects should consider the use of **Trusted Platform Module** (**TPM**) and **Trusted Execution Environment** (**TEE**) technologies, when possible, to aid in ensuring the identity and ownership of the hardware device.

These technologies can also be used to establish the ownership of devices and automate the transfer of ownership. The **Fast IDentity Online** (**FIDO**) Alliance created the **FIDO Device Onboard** (**FDO**) specification in 2019 to standardize this hands-free onboarding process. Intel Corporation then created an open source project named FDO to provide tools and an SDK and implementation example so that organizations could easily create solutions that complied with the specification. FDO works with TPM and TEE technologies.

The process begins when device manufacturers create an ownership voucher before shipping the device. When the user activates the device, the other half of the authentication process is completed, making the device operationally secure. See *Figure 7.5* for an overview of the ownership transfer process following the FDO specification.

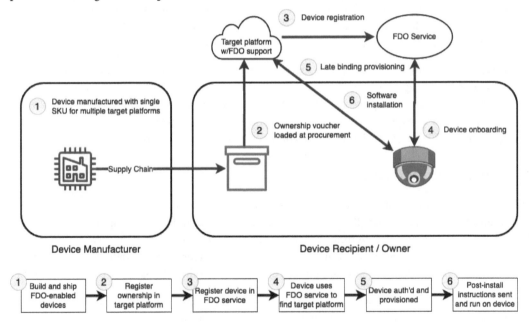

Figure 7.5 - Provisioning a device with FDO

Open Horizon's support for the FDO project can be found at `https://github.com/open-horizon/FDO-support/blob/main/README.md`. There is a GitHub repository (`https://github.com/open-horizon/FDO-support`) where the corresponding integration software between FDO and Open Horizon can be found.

Trusted data

Here we will list various solution components that will enable operational data security and show how they can be combined.

In the *Data encryption* section of *Chapter 6*, we discussed the concept of a **Data Confidence Fabric (DCF)** and how it can generate data confidence scores to give you a level of confidence that you understand the source of the data, how it may have been manipulated or altered, and how likely it is that the data has or has not been subject to undetected tampering.

Likewise, in the same section, we covered a technique that allows calculations to be performed on encrypted data without first decrypting it, and the results delivered are encrypted. That technique, **fully homomorphic encryption** (**FHE**), should be considered in any architecture where the data being collected is numeric and sensitive, confidential, or regulated.

In *Chapter 3*, we briefly mentioned the concept of perfect forward secrecy, where two parties communicating over an encrypted protocol (such as TLS 1.3) can then further encrypt messages using asymmetric public key encryption so the receiver can decrypt the message using their private key and the sender's public key, with the session being encrypted using a key unique to that session. The strength of this approach is that in the off chance the session can be intercepted and decrypted by a third party, the key used to decrypt that session cannot also be used to decrypt messages between those parties sent in any other session.

Trusted compute

We've talked about trusted data, trusted hardware, limiting connectivity, and other security-related features that businesses like to see before embarking on an edge solution. It all adds up to this paradigm of **trusted edge computing** (**TEC**), which strives for the next level of security of running secure and isolated containers, secure storage, and even secure memory. It also addresses business application protection mechanisms running on edge infrastructures. The solution architect must assure enterprises that their data, their program logic, and, ultimately, their intellectual property are protected. That should ideally involve remote attestation of business logic running on edge devices.

Running an application in a container provides some resource isolation, but it does not provide the sort of security isolation of identity or network isolation that you get when using VMs. Hence, you have to take advantage of the different layers of a container platform. *Figure 7.6* shows the various layers, which put together provide the required security isolation and trust.

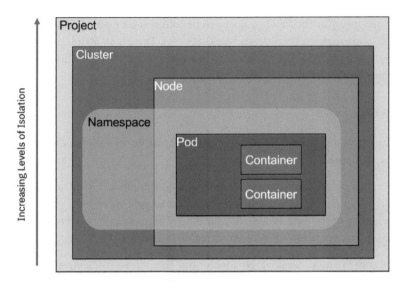

Figure 7.6 - Isolation provided by Kubernetes layers

As an example, Kubernetes has different layers that are nested. If you start from the smallest unit, the container on the inside, and move out, the level of isolation and security progressively increases. Container technology is one option. There could be other alternatives but the reason we focus on containers is that many edge applications are by their very nature more suited to run in containers.

Tactical Edge

Tactical Edge is a term that describes secure edge computing in contested environments where different entities across different domains are vying for similar resources. It combines the best practices of operational security in edge computing working in tandem with a secure edge platform. Further, its default operating assumptions are geared toward both offline-first principles as well as **denied, disrupted, and intermittent connectivity with limited bandwidth** (DDIL). Let's briefly describe what system components go into a Tactical Edge platform architecture, define their operational characteristics, and then discuss ways to automate the provisioning and operation of Tactical Edge environments.

Tactical Edge consists of hardware and software working together as a unified solution to support mission-critical workloads in field-deployed environments outside the core network and cloud infrastructure. It should do the following:

- Operate in disrupted, disconnected, denied, degraded, intermittent, or limited communication environments

- Function in degraded or otherwise extreme environmental conditions and operating environments

- Be self-sustaining as long as possible

- Be built as ruggedized units and maintained with **commercial off-the-shelf** (**COTS**), open source, and custom-built technologies

- Be deployable at scale, usable, and accessible in the field by anyone, in adverse conditions, and with minimal training

Attributes and elements of the Tactical Edge include the following:

- Trusted infrastructure, computers, devices, data, models, and identities

- Small-footprint devices, including both compute and wearables

- Runtime protection with zero trust

- Secure, redundant communication capabilities

- Resilient operation, yet breakable if removed from a specified geofence

> **Note**
> Geofence is a technology that uses location services to enforce or activate a virtual boundary.

- Deployable and replaceable in minutes without IT or OT staff, including zero touch

> **Note**
> Zero-touch deployment is the ability to remotely provision edge devices without having to do it manually. The zero-touch paradigm is discussed in *Chapter 9*.

- Capable of running on-demand analytics and sensor fusion use cases adapted to local capacity

- Capable of bursting northbound for extra capacity

A Tactical Edge platform that meets the requirements listed previously is built on compute hardware that employs zero trust from the silicon on up, with a hardware-based root of trust for platform attestation, workload signing, and confidence-scoring injection into a data confidence fabric. Running on that hardware should be a Kubernetes distribution, integrated to provide hardware-based workload isolation and protection from competing workloads. Together, the two provide data protection at rest, in motion, and while processing. Additionally, a secure, pull-based workload and ML model life cycle management solution should be employed to handle placement and deployment tasks. Also, on top of that, a secure, redundant network overlay should be deployed and run.

> **Note**
>
> *From the silicon on up* means visualizing the stack or architecture of a computer from the physical layer (motherboard, processing units, and memory) up to the operating system and/or virtualization layer to the running applications. It's not enough to secure the applications if the operating system is not secure. And it's not enough to secure the operating system if the hardware has vulnerabilities. By securing the complete system, beginning with the hardware, you ensure you've presented the smallest potential attack surface possible.

Such an environment fits scenarios where the operating climate is harsh and stressful with restricted communication networks. See *Figure 7.7*. Some examples are ground operations on a battlefield, a fleet of merchant ships or aircraft carriers facing challenging weather at sea, and disaster response teams in disaster areas, where solutions must be resilient to disruption and sometimes survival is based on distributed decision-making.

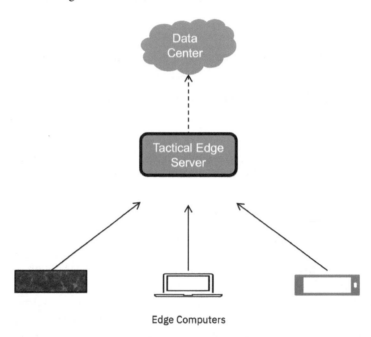

Figure 7.7 - Tactical Edge components

By using secure hardware compute and devices that support FDO technology for provisioning, hardware can complete all day 1 tasks over local networks or be pre-provisioned elsewhere and then deployed locally for scenarios and locations with no local connectivity. This approach will meet all of the preceding Tactical Edge considerations: zero-touch and zero-trust operation by minimally trained people in the field using COTS hardware.

In the next section, we will discuss scenarios based on how the use of AI can optimize automation.

Automation with AI

We discussed deploying AI applications and ML models at the edge in *Chapter 5*, which is becoming a common scenario because enterprises are adamant about reducing the time for decision-making and minimizing data movement. In *Chapter 4*, we touched upon using AI/ML applications to determine network traffic patterns and using automation to perform network maintenance and monitor network performance. This latter discussion, albeit brief, is more in keeping with the automation theme.

Using AI techniques to automate facets of the edge computing paradigm will allow for automation at scale. With so much data being generated by edge devices, enterprises are finding ways to not only infer and analyze that data but also create a corpus that can be used to learn from, build, and train new models. We now see the rise of such corpus models as **Large Language Models** (**LLMs**).

LLMs and generative AI

LLMs are massive amounts of data gathered from numerous existing sources that can be used to answer natural language queries, perform summarizations, or create classifications. These ML models that use neural networks are trained on massive amounts of data and can predict the next word in a natural language sentence. LLMs are a subset of **generative AI** (**GenAI**).

These models and techniques have given rise to a new form of AI, namely GenAI. As the name suggests, this category of AI models can generate new and previously unseen content, including text, music, and images. From an edge computing perspective, the best use case of GenAI is image processing.

LLMs and GenAI stem from **foundation models** (**FMs**), which are any model trained on very large data from the web using ML. They contain what are called tunable parameters in a mathematical sense, which ends up being their unit of size. When a model is listed as 3B, it means the model contains 3 billion tunable parameters. Although the terms LLM and FM are often used interchangeably, they are different because FMs can be more than just linguistic models. *Figure 7.8* depicts which of the model types could be more relevant in the domain of edge computing.

> **Parameter**
> A parameter is a configuration variable inside the model that can be tuned to optimize its performance.

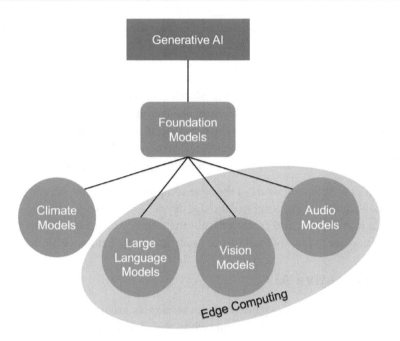

Figure 7.8 - FMs and LLMs in Edge Computing

We have seen drones used in industrial settings where they are deployed to assess and inspect an area or equipment. Imagine a drone sent to inspect a large concrete bridge to look for cracks or other structural variations. In the traditional world of AI, it would be limited to a small set of historical data, specifically images, to ascertain whether a linear marking is a crack or not. A human would have to determine whether it was indeed a crack after further analysis.

But now the drone can use the power of GenAI and compare what it is *seeing* to data contained in these large FMs to determine on its own whether something is a crack or a fault in the concrete structure. Using data from those large models improves the performance of visual analysis. Industry-specific vision models can be applied in different scenarios to get quicker and better results.

Using AI in automation

The challenge lies in using all these AI domains to automate tasks and help OT and IT with managing and monitoring edge devices, clusters, and network components. Thanks to FMs, it is possible to automate the drone scenario of detecting faults or defects in industrial scenarios. That would possibly require less human intervention and mitigate errors in such scenarios.

Another example of where GenAI could play a major role in edge solutions is in responding to questions from customers as in the case of directional kiosks. This would take advantage of the question-and-answer capability of LLMs. Based on what the customer is enquiring about, the system could anticipate the customer's next question and suggest things. Similarly, **quick service restaurants** (**QSRs**) could look at replacing order takers at drive-throughs with AI systems backed by GenAI, specifically the natural language processing capability. Taking the customer's order, recommending add-ons, and speeding up the entire process is another example of automation with AI.

Automating with AI is a bit more obvious when dealing with the network because we can use historical data to determine network traffic patterns and use AI to automate network maintenance and help it perform better. As an example, this would really help in determining how to slice a 5G network, which can be a complex task. When it comes to **multi-access edge computing** (**MEC**), IaC can be an essential tool to facilitate their deployments. Furthermore, with the load that MEC could experience, it is important to continually monitor the demand and optimize all its services. Demand monitoring and auto-scaling could be achieved with automation, specifically automation using AI.

IEEE published a survey about automated application deployment on MEC that be found here (`https://ieeexplore.ieee.org/document/10225499`).

Section II describes MEC and provides a reference architecture. *Section III* describes the various IaC tools and compares them, including Ansible and Terraform.

Summary

The chapter started with a discussion of service delivery automation, which is a rather broad term for automating human tasks in a business and is relevant to edge computing. Whether it is DevOps or IaC, achieving scalability through automation ends up being one of the major benefits. We saw that from monitoring edge devices to updating the applications and models running on those devices, there is an opportunity to apply automation.

The latter half of the chapter addressed the security aspect by introducing the onboarding of edge devices with security features before shipping them. While it seemed like we digressed, it was important to talk about security in the context of automation. Automation allows enterprises to build capabilities that can react with minimal human interaction in a more secure and trusted way.

The final section dealt with the most interesting and relevant topic, namely AI. It seems AI is omnipresent in edge computing from AI applications deployed on edge devices to the use of AI in the deployment of devices and their operation. Enterprises can now look ahead to the use of FMs in edge computing.

While we have briefly mentioned monitoring in this chapter, *Chapter 8* takes a deeper look into the domain of observability.

8

Monitoring and Observability

As Peter Drucker once said, "*You can't improve what you don't measure.*" Edge devices are often deployed in remote environments with minimal to no presence of IT operations teams, making monitoring and troubleshooting rather challenging. No matter how remote, enterprises need to maintain and protect their infrastructure, and that requires remote monitoring to manage their distributed assets.

The irony here is that edge computing solutions are typically used to monitor other systems, be it in stores, warehouses, or shop floors, or during manufacturing processes. So, who is monitoring the edge computing system, which is usually a combined hardware and software solution topology?

In an edge computing solution, there are many components to be monitored, from the application to the infrastructure. Components include edge hubs, servers and hosts, systems, network components, edge applications, and AI/ML models

In this chapter, monitoring and observability from an edge computing perspective are discussed to ensure that a deployed edge solution is performing as designed. Of all the components we focus on, the network and connectivity are critical due to their unique characteristics. Any monitoring solution must provide enterprises with the opportunity to measure the performance of the edge solution and, if needed, make improvements. Thus, these related topics are addressed:

- Monitoring and observability
- Measuring to improve
- What to measure

Monitoring and observability

In the previous chapter, we talked about the need for automation to update applications with minimal human interaction. Monitoring, similarly, is key to knowing that edge devices are working properly and that the applications and models deployed on those devices are running. Note that there are two aspects: the physical hardware and the deployed software. The hardware in this case includes not only the various edge devices but also the edge hubs/servers.

Although sometimes used interchangeably, there are subtle differences between monitoring and observability. Based on our findings, in *Table 8.1*, we list some of the differences between the two:

Monitoring	Observability
Reactive in nature, collecting logs	Proactively interpreting collected data
Is the system working?	What is the system doing?
Collection of metrics, events, logs	Deals with traces
What is the state of the system?	Why is the system in the current state?
Indicates when something is wrong	Tells you why something is wrong
Enables observability	Requires more than monitoring

Table 8.1 – Differences between monitoring and observability

While monitoring is reactive and collects logs, observability is proactively interpreting the data that has been collected. A **log** is an information about an event in a human-readable format. The measurement of that event, in the unit related to that event, is a **metric**. The relationship between two or more events is known as **tracing**. These three types of captured event records form the basis of observability, as shown in *Figure 8.1*. Observability is in some sense a superset of monitoring:

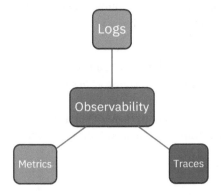

Figure 8.1 – The three components of observability

Observability is not unique to IT practice. It is actually an engineering term used in control systems. These could be applied to systems on the shop floor, in automobiles, or in any complex system that requires diagnostics to determine when something has gone wrong. From an edge computing perspective, observability allows enterprises to proactively detect, troubleshoot, and resolve issues, optimize performance, and ensure the reliable operation of edge devices. A solution architect must anticipate that customers will also enquire about network observability because they would want to ensure that the network is operating optimally.

How monitoring works

It is important to constantly assess the health of a system. That is done by collecting data and writing those data records to logs. That is what monitoring is all about—measuring the health of applications, watching a system's performance, creating alerts, and detecting failures. However, the value of monitoring really shows when developers and operations staff work together and determine the metrics to gather and what to log. There has to be a balance between logging too much and not logging enough.

How observability works

With the metrics and logs collected, the next task is to analyze what has been collected and correlate data from several sources. When a problem occurs, observability would indicate why the problem happened. A good observability platform would not only detect the failure but even suggest remediation. An intelligent platform would go one step further and remediate the issue in order to maintain the promised **service-level objective (SLO)**.

> **Additional information**
> An SLO is a specific metric within a **service-level agreement (SLA)**, such as 99.99% uptime.

Of late. we see **artificial intelligence (AI)** and **machine learning (ML)** being incorporated into observability platforms to detect anomalies and surface predictive insights. This is especially true of network observability.

How network observability works

Monitoring edge devices and edge applications and observing how they perform is the obvious part of edge computing. But, remember, the network is crucial in an edge solution. The **network operations (NetOps)** folks are constantly monitoring the network. Given that today's networks are so complex due to the combination of hardware and software components and that they generate so much data, total network observability by humans is near impossible. It is left to intelligent observability software platforms to maintain complete situational awareness of the network.

The three main components of network observability are shown in *Figure 8.2* – telemetry data from various sources in the network, a data platform that can ingest the telemetry data for analysis, and the ability to take corrective action:

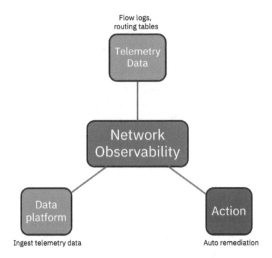

Figure 8.2 – The three components of network observability

Watching how the network is functioning, predicting trends in network traffic, and (above all) ensuring service assurance is what network observability is all about. And now, with new technologies such as **network function virtualization** (**NFV**), 5G, network slicing, and the dynamic nature of networks, using AI is essential when it comes to observability.

There are many monitoring and alerting tools that enterprises can use. Some of the common open source software tools are listed here in alphabetical order. This is by no means an exhaustive list:

- Fluentd (`https://github.com/fluent/fluentd`)
- Grafana (`https://grafana.com/grafana/`)
- Graphite (`https://github.com/graphite-project`)
- Nagios (`https://www.nagios.org/`)
- Prometheus (`https://prometheus.io/`)
- SkyWalking (`https://skywalking.apache.org/`)
- Zabbix (`https://www.zabbix.com/`)

Measuring to improve

Performance optimization, threat detection and mitigation, and ensuring reliable operation of any system, including edge solutions, is the ultimate goal of monitoring and observability. All the collection of metrics and logging and setting up alerts will not amount to much if the gathered information is not used to do **root cause analysis** (**RCA**) and fix what is wrong or improve a system's performance. In that context, dashboards play an important role in the observability domain.

Dashboards should help with visualizing curated data, providing context, and offering a holistic view over time rather than at just a point in time. By displaying graphs and trend lines along with the actual metrics, dashboards help humans see the history of the data and the impact of an alarm when it occurred, and, most importantly, they add context and reason. Note that alarms should only be set for things that are important and they should be actionable.

Network observability example

We are starting to see how 5G is transforming sporting events for spectators by providing immersive experiences. Notwithstanding the costs, 5G connectivity allows fans to watch the event from multiple angles on different handheld devices and even indulge in **augmented reality** (**AR**). While the business outcome is a wonderful experience for the fans and spectators, the **communications service provider** (**CSP**) having to offer these services has to work very hard in the networking realm.

From the organizer's perspective, the solution architect would have to work closely with the network engineers from the CSP and make many architectural decisions. This would involve making infrastructure-related decisions regarding equipment in and around the stadium, such as how many 5G towers, **multi-access edge computing** (**MEC**) nodes, and private 5G cores there should be, and more. Then, there would be network-related decisions to be made regarding the CSP, such as the amount of bandwidth to provide, how many network slices to allocate to the event, how to synchronize various camera feeds, etc. *Figure 8.3* attempts to capture some of the network-slicing aspects during a large stadium event. Another option could be to use private 5G within the stadium:

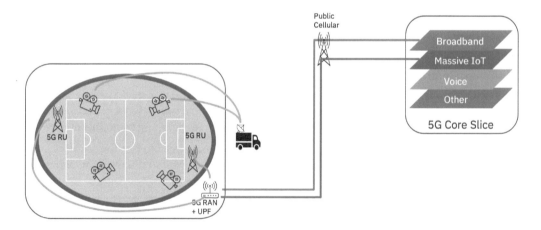

Figure 8.3 – CSP offering network services at a stadium event

Not all of the above-mentioned architectural decisions are static, one-time decisions. The network team would have to observe the network traffic and be ready to scale. As bandwidth demand increases, the system would have to dedicate more network slices to the event. These types of actions, based on traffic demand, metrics, and thresholds, are best done with AI-enhanced software because they can be tuned to anticipate and predict trends. The system would measure response times and the number of subscribers, seeing how spectators are interacting with the services, noting weather conditions, and taking corrective actions, all in real time so that the CSP can maintain the promised SLAs. The goal of monitoring and observability systems is to provide insights into resource utilization and data feeds and prevent any sort of hiccups. All this is done to ensure spectators at the event have a fantastic experience.

What to measure

There are certain network-related metrics that help NetOps teams maintain the network uptime and then there are some infrastructure elements that need to be closely observed.

Real user monitoring

In the stadium scenario, we mentioned the NetOps team would monitor how spectators were interacting with the services. That would require **real-time user monitoring** (**RUM**) data as opposed to synthetic or historical data. Getting a real-time view of what users are experiencing online is critical because the NetOps team needs to analyze events as they are happening and proactively look into slow connections or fix any misconfigurations.

Monitoring software can use RUM data to make DNS routing and other network traffic-steering decisions. There is also intelligent traffic steering, which is usually implemented using the overlay network.

> **Additional information**
>
> **Synthetic data** is different from real-world data. It is annotated data created using computer simulations and algorithms. It is artificial data from the digital world, but it reflects the real world. Synthetic data is used for training AI models, which requires large amounts of data.
>
> **Synthetic monitoring** is something that development teams use to test the features and performance of applications by simulating user actions. It is meant to discover any potential errors and have them fixed before an end user encounters them.
>
> Synthetic monitoring can be used to improve network performance.

Network performance management

Whether it is a physical network or a software-defined network, monitoring its performance is what NetOps teams do. Performance data is collected using polling and other network streaming telemetry, so organizations can analyze and use graphing software to view it.

Some of the factors that affect a network's performance are as follows:

- **Number of devices**: From an edge computing perspective, any network should be able to handle hundreds and thousands of devices.

- **Bandwidth**: This is the amount of data transmitted over a certain amount of time. New technologies such as 5G have vastly improved network bandwidth.

- **Throughput**: This depends on bandwidth and is a measure of the number of messages successfully sent through the network over a certain amount of time.

- **Network latency**: Given the remoteness of devices, network latency is the biggest concern. Network latency is basically the measure of how long it takes for a message to be transmitted across the network from one endpoint to the next. Remember, latency is affected by the number of devices on the network and the type of devices.

Most **network performance management** (**NPM**) software measures these basic metrics and a lot more, and they can present the information in simple dashboards. Network infrastructure and the type of edge applications used in the network affect network performance.

Anomaly detection

Any value or event that is out of the ordinary or an outlier in a set of data is considered an anomaly. Anomaly detection is an important tool in network troubleshooting and intrusion detection systems. It is usually done by analyzing traffic flow patterns and network packets to uncover any hidden threats or intrusions. Network monitoring has to be done 24/7, and that is better done by an automated system. When an anomaly is detected, it should be mitigated or autocorrected or the NetOps team should be immediately notified. This is critical in maintaining network security.

Capacity

Observing how the system performs over a period of time helps predict resource demands and even identify capacity gaps. That is true in network monitoring as well as for other infrastructure. Is the network able to handle the deluge of data from the edge devices? If the edge hub/server cannot keep up with the amount of data being generated by the edge devices, the monitoring and system should proactively adjust compute and even storage resources to maintain optimal edge solution performance.

Business outcomes

Thus far we talked about the various technology-related measurements and metrics. Those become important because they directly or indirectly affect business outcomes. The common business drivers that enterprises focus on are as follows:

- **Customer experience**: Maintaining an optimally operating system improves customer experience. If the system is not performing well, it eventually affects the customer and adversely affects customer satisfaction.

- **Regulatory compliance**: Whether it is via traceability, audit logging, or security-related metrics, observability helps with meeting regulatory requirements. Through constant observance, the system must help maintain security and privacy standards.

- **Risk mitigation**: Continuous and automated observability can aid in identifying potential risks early and taking proactive mitigation measures. This would reduce the impacts of such risks, which could be expensive.

Improving edge solution

In this section, we describe some of the monitoring challenges caused by the unique nature of edge topologies. To overcome these challenges and improve the performance of such edge solutions, the solution architect must be aware of how the designed solution should operate and how it is operating. There are the infrastructure components in the solution and there are edge applications running on those components. Different personas are interested in knowing how the two are performing - the Ops team and the developers.

Monitoring challenges at the edge

It might seem obvious, but the operations team must review the current solution and take stock of the current state of all the components involved, especially the network components. Then, they must understand what the desired state is and get insights across all the components. In most cases, this should all be done in real time so that changes can be made without any interruption of service.

We mentioned the uniqueness of edge solutions. Its uniqueness lies in its ability to operate in disconnected mode. Hence, the challenge then becomes monitoring edge devices when they're operating in disconnected or offline mode. **Disconnected**, or **offline**, means that the devices are operating but do not have connections to the enterprise or the cloud for a certain period of time. That means end-to-end metrics won't be collected but operating logs will continue to be written locally. The system should be designed so that when full connectivity is restored, all local data will be uploaded and synced up automatically and the collection of metrics will resume. See a typical deployment in *Figure 8.4*:

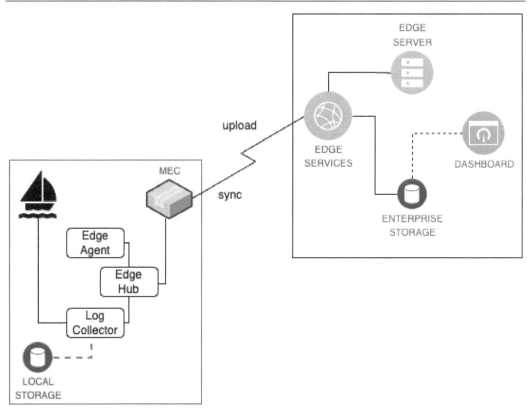

Figure 8.4 – Edge monitoring in disconnected mode

In general, the question is what is the right way to measure and report on autonomous edge devices such as ships, space-borne devices, and even autonomous vehicles when they are disconnected or offline? The recommendation is to plan for offline operations and continue with local logging and monitoring. When the opportunity arises for them to be reconnected, immediately reconnect them and upload and sync all the data with the enterprise system.

Configuration changes at the edge

Observability is not always about how the system is performing or why it is not performing. It is possible that the system is not performing the way it is supposed to because there is a configuration change, either planned or unplanned. If a device is physically moved, is inoperable, or was configured incorrectly, then a connectivity component pointing to a nonexistent endpoint could break things in the edge application. Hence, configuration changes should be part of the observability solution, and observability dashboards should help correlate configuration changes with possible system errors, even if the cause is an edge device being inadvertently tampered with. The challenge for any edge computing operations team is to determine why a remote edge device is not online.

Edge application monitoring

By design, we have focused on infrastructure monitoring because, in our opinion, infrastructure plays a major role in IoT/edge solutions. That doesn't minimize the importance of applications and AI models running on edge devices. While these models and applications seem to have fewer variations, they nevertheless should be monitored.

Similar to NPM, there is **application performance monitoring** (**APM**): a process for monitoring the performance of applications. APM is meant to help IT professionals ensure that the deployed applications are performing reliably as designed. In edge computing, real-time APM is critical because it helps you identify issues before they have a major impact on the designed solution. The common metrics that APM tracks are CPU usage, memory usage, disk usage, response times, application uptime, and error rate.

Given that edge computing applications are typically cloud-native and container-based, there are other metrics that are more relevant, such as node availability, container start times, input/output data rates, number of instances, cloud costs, and APIs called. As was mentioned earlier, monitoring is critical because, either directly or indirectly, it affects business outcomes.

Personas

There are certain personas that are closely involved and interested in the monitoring and observability of IT solutions. They are **site reliability engineers** (**SREs**), IT administrators, and NetOps and DevOps teams. Since edge solutions often use AI models to analyze data, we think AI and data scientists are the other personas that should keep an eye on those dashboards.

As a solution architect, one ought to take a holistic view and ensure that the monitoring dashboards are (a) customizable and (b) accessible to every team in the enterprise that has a stake in the solution. Based on our experience, in *Table 8.2*, we list some of the tasks that each of the personas would be responsible for. The business user persona is also listed because, ultimately, this is the persona benefitting from these monitoring and observability efforts. Enterprises may have additional roles or decide to combine a couple of them:

Persona	Tasks
SRE	Monitor the availability of the system
	Monitor alerts and critical incidents
	Identify the root causes of issues that arise
IT admin	Track resource usage and optimize capacity
	Respond to outages
	Manage SLOs

DevOps	Monitor application performance
	Obtain release and pipeline feedback
NetOps	Monitor network performance
	Watch for and respond to network outages
	Monitor network anomalies
Data engineer	Monitor the performance of models
	Watch for model drift and model retraining
Business user	Track the overall health of the system
	Monitor business-defined SLAs

Table 8.2 – Observability personas and tasks

Additionally, a solution architect should actively look for how the information in the dashboards is consumed. If an automation step can be added, especially through judicious application of AI, propose that. Anytime you can shorten the **observe, orient, decide, act** (**OODA**) loop, you reduce your enterprise's time to act, thus increasing responsiveness and decreasing costs. Ask yourself this: why are we collecting this data, how will we use the data, and what possible responses can we choose based on the data? Those are your automation opportunities.

Summary

If monitoring actively collects data by way of logs and metrics, observability applies intelligence to make sense of the collected data and provide actionable insights. The chapter listed the differences between the two and pointed to the fact that monitoring and observability complement each other to help solve problems in the IT world. The same is true in edge computing. The end goal should be to dynamically and continuously improve the overall efficiency of the edge computing infrastructure. If you find an area in your processes where observability is not currently implemented, consider addressing that gap at your next opportunity.

What to measure and measuring to improve were discussed in the latter part of the chapter. This highlighted the opportunity gap: enterprises should know the current state and desired state of the edge solution. Only by continuously monitoring the system can enterprises achieve the desired state, and that drives operational maturity. Lastly, application performance monitoring was discussed.

In *Chapter 9*, the connectivity aspects of an edge solution will be described, which is a natural extension to maintaining the desired state.

9

Connect Judiciously but Thoughtlessly

There are three common and potentially overlapping scenarios when connecting applications and services to each other and to fixed infrastructure services: connecting within a secure trusted network behind a **DMZ (Demilitarized Zone, a perimeter network)**, connecting over an untrusted network, and connecting over a transitory or unstable network, whether trusted or not. Each organization involved in providing or enabling that access will have its own processes for provisioning and managing that connectivity. However, all of them serve a purpose orthogonal to the needs of an application architecture.

This chapter discusses a point of view for connectivity that begins and ends with the needs of the application and those that maintain it to optimize the speed and agility of developers and **SRE** (**Site Reliability Engineering**, IT Operations using software engineering practices) professionals.

In this chapter, we will cover the following main topics:

- Declarative versus imperative configuration
- Zero Trust or as close as you can get
- Overlay, underlay, and shared responsibilities

By the end of this chapter, you will understand the benefits of application-directed networking and the potential value it can bring to an enterprise by bridging operational silos and abstracting proprietary cloud vendor-offering interfaces and network underlays.

Suggested pre-reading material

If you would like to learn more about the topics we will discuss, the following resources are recommended:

- Application-centric infrastructure: `https://venturebeat.com/business/what-is-application-centric-infrastructure/`

- Application-centric networking: `https://www.ibm.com/blog/application-centric-networking-for-the-modern-enterprise-era/`

- Zero Trust explained: `https://www.youtube.com/watch?v=yn6CPQ9RioA`

- NIST Special Publication 800-207, *Zero Trust Architecture*: `https://nvlpubs.nist.gov/nistpubs/SpecialPublications/NIST.SP.800-207.pdf`

Declarative versus imperative configuration

In this section, you will learn about approaches to, and tools for, configuring your edge-connected networks that will increase deployment velocity while removing barriers and bottlenecks. We will give an example from the emerging field of application-centric, or application-directed, networking. By the end, you will be able to explain the benefits of this paradigm and consider when to use it for your distributed edge application architectures.

Comparing the two approaches

Cloud Foundry and other platforms introduced, and Kubernetes popularized, the idea of marrying declarative configurations describing the desired outcome state to the concept of eventual consistency, thus bringing a system gradually into alignment from the current state toward the eventual goals. The declarative paradigm is a way of stating (with configuration files or a higher-order language) the outcome that you would like to achieve *without needing to specify how to do so*. This gives the implementation of the solution the flexibility to determine whether the target system or environment already matches that stated outcome, or whether changes need to be made to bring it into correspondence with that end goal.

The imperative approach, by contrast, specifies specific operations to be performed in the specified order without an understanding of the current system state or the administrator's eventual goals. This produces brittle solutions that can easily fail when they hardcode assumptions about an operating environment and its participants. These imperative configurations can also lack validation checks and enforcement of full life cycle coverage unless those are also specifically anticipated and covered. This leads to boilerplate code/configuration inflation and a *push-and-forget* mentality that assumes the task is complete once the tool has run without throwing errors. Every subsequent modification to that configuration or code requires a human to modify it, test the updates, and then push the resulting assets into production.

In edge computing, when you are dealing with so many different architectures, operating systems, and hardware devices, using an imperative approach to configuration introduces risk by specifying precise, static steps to take that may very well be environment- and microarchitecture-specific. This is why edge-native best practices work best with tools and solutions that use a declarative approach to configuration and allow the tool to dynamically determine the best way to achieve the desired outcome. It abstracts away the complexity and differences from one application host and environment to another. See *Table 9.1* for the authors' high-level summary directly comparing the approaches.

Declarative Programming	Imperative Programming
Describes the desired result with no direction on how to achieve it	Describes how to accomplish the desired result
Specifies what is to be done	Specifies how it is to be done
Variables are usually immutable	Variables could be mutable
Code optimized by the system based on constraints created by the programmer	Code optimization is the responsibility of the programmer
Details are largely hidden or minimized from the developer's view	Developers have a lot of control, which is important in low-level programming

Table 9.1 – Declarative programming contrasted with the imperative approach

With these two approaches in mind, let's discuss the barriers and bottlenecks faced by modern enterprises when it comes to placing and connecting applications to services, other applications, and infrastructure.

What slows down application deployment on the edge?

In an enterprise, CloudOps or NetOps (the terms, and team responsibilities, are sometimes interchangeable in this context) is responsible for providing secure, performant connectivity for applications wherever they are located to the resources they are connecting to. DevOps is responsible for the **continuous integration and continuous deployment (CI/CD)** pipelines, which place the workloads and related assets at their destination and connect them to their resources and dependencies. It is incumbent on DevOps to communicate with CloudOps about the workload connectivity requirements, and then wait for CloudOps to provision the requested connectivity with the appropriate access control restrictions in place.

This back-and-forth can take weeks to complete and will need to be performed for all environments: development, testing, and production. Additionally, the process will need to be repeated for any modifications to existing deployed workloads, and for workload removal.

If a system or tool is misconfigured or otherwise does not function properly in production, it requires collaboration between the CloudOps and DevOps teams to analyze the situation, perform a **root cause analysis (RCA)**, and then request the appropriate changes to fix the issue(s). However, it is quite possible that existing observability and monitoring tools do not provide enough information to determine the root cause without back-and-forth experimentation and testing. This leads to a very long time being spent with all teams addressing discovered problems.

One other issue is that this **slow-motion communication and configuration change process** prevents the ability of either team to allow the solution to adapt itself rapidly and dynamically to changing environmental factors, whether cost- or performance-based. In other words, it prevents **dynamic freedom of movement**.

In summary, two or more different teams are responsible for different types of tasks:

- Deploying applications efficiently without error
- (Dynamically) connecting applications securely with good performance and within budget

The tools at their disposal are only designed and optimized for those specific tasks and views and do not translate well to other domains and those domains' terminology, leading to potential communication issues when troubleshooting. And the teams are not incentivized to help other teams meet their KPIs, nor to provide methods and processes to make the other team's tasks quicker and easier to accomplish. See *Figure 9.1* for a comparison of the two approaches and how the latter application-centric approach allows responsibilities to be shifted left.

The Traditional Siloed Approach

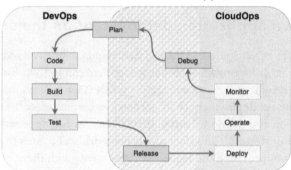

The Application Centered Approach

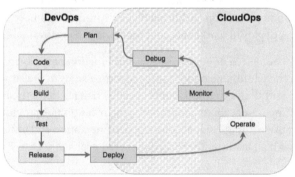

Figure 9.1 – Application life cycle management responsibilities compared

If a type of solution could provide DevOps with a self-service function when it comes to network connectivity, as shown in the lower diagram of *Figure 9.1*, while still allowing CloudOps to have granular control over the when/where/what policies and rules of that connectivity, that would go a long way toward improving the status quo. Additionally, it would need to provide enhanced tools and dashboards to expose the state of the workloads and networks and allow "what if" scenarios to be proposed and tested. It would need to allow CloudOps to delegate some execution authority to the DevOps team to be able to make isolated changes to network overlays (and sometimes underlays) specific to the workloads being remediated without potentially disrupting any other activities on the network underlays. Lastly, it should provide the capability to implement dynamic automation so the configuration, and resulting workload deployments, could react to changing conditions by moving and scaling seamlessly.

Let's break the problem down into specific approaches that will help you better solve the aforementioned issues and proposed solution requirements.

Solutioning edge-connected networks and applications

Eight best practice approaches are listed here that address those issues for workloads deployed to the edge in a hybrid, multi-cloud world, ideally using declarative configuration:

- *Any solution you choose should be abstracted from any physical hardware or vendor-specific APIs.* By using a tool, interface, or API that is vendor- and solution-agnostic, you avoid the trap of specifying your desired outcome(s) as a series of "do this and then that" imperative steps that must be followed in an inflexible sequence. This frees you to instead list the outcomes to be achieved, and in order if required. It also allows you to use vendor-neutral language or terms to describe those outcomes so that you do not accidentally use vendor-specific meanings, overloaded words, or vague terminology. It also gives you flexibility and freedom of movement by ensuring that you are not locked into a specific vendor, platform, or paradigm.

- *Your solutions should rely on auto-discovery of network underlays and related infrastructure, namespaces, policies, ACLs, applications, services, and platforms.* Few individuals in a company know how to connect to multiple cloud vendor platforms, query the information, and then consolidate all of that in an easy-to-understand format. By using a solution that can provide that capability, you increase your CloudOps team's capacity to respond to requests and allow the team members to focus on higher-value tasks. Furthermore, there's the issue of providing access (and maintaining that access) to individuals who need the information. Instead, organizations are bottlenecked by requesting the information from those who have it, assuming they receive the information they need in the first response. Instead, by having a single solution that is provided with read-only access to all cloud resources, you can then provide access to that solution to any person in the organization who needs the results. A self-service platform could provide many, if not all, of these capabilities. However, adding the auto-discovery of resources to this mix reduces initial setup and ongoing maintenance times from days to hours or even minutes.

- *Your solutions should be able to dynamically reconfigure network infrastructure within the bounds of CloudOps-controlled and -specified guardrails.* If a DevOps team member needs a reasonable change made to enable their workload to function, and it does not interfere with existing and planned network usage, and the changes are capable of being automated, then that type of change is safe to perform. If that work can further be delegated to a tool that will validate the configuration parameters and implement the change without error, then it is safer to have the tool perform the update than it would be for a human.

- *Any solution you choose should be able to dynamically provision and modify an application-connected network overlay.* This is another task that would typically be performed by a CloudOps team. However, it also requires detailed, error-free communication and advanced planning between teams to work out what should happen, to schedule times when all parties are available to perform the work without impacting the production environment or causing unreasonable downtime, and then testing time afterward to ensure it was correctly performed and has the desired outcome. If your solution can automate all of those steps safely and without error, then it speeds up rollouts while also reducing the potential for errors and the expense of all of the workers it would normally require. A solution that can do this more than pays for itself.

- *Your solutions should be application-aware and application-centric.* This capability ensures that applications, services, infrastructure, and related resources exist and are where they are supposed to be. It also determines how they are configured (including access controls), what the software versions are, and what resources they are accessing (both physical and virtual), and then surfaces that information so that it can be consumed by other tools and solutions. Without this capability, humans would have to perform all those actions flawlessly every single time.

- *Your preferred solutions should be able to operate autonomously.* There are several reasons for this requirement. With the appropriate configuration, a tool is more than capable of achieving the outcome, so why have a person manually follow the steps? More importantly, the steps will need to be performed on remote systems, and by ensuring that only your tool has access to the target systems, you reduce the potential attack surface and do not need to update which persons need access to which systems as your organization experiences normal employee turnover. And with no human in the loop, you can ensure that the tasks can be performed at any time.

- *Your solutions should be integrated with real-time observability and monitoring solutions.* When you use declarative configuration in conjunction with automated and autonomous solutions, you ensure that tasks are performed consistently and correctly every time. But if you are also able to add information about the operating environment, application and network performance, and all potential resources, you level up your capabilities. This means that your deployments can respond to changing conditions and situations to match the desired operating targets more closely. It will also give you the ability to consider and test "what if" scenarios to iteratively improve and optimize application performance.

- *Any solutions you choose should enable zero-touch, hands-free operation.* This is the last, critical step in removing **human-in-the-loop** (**HITL**) interactions to prevent errors and reduce operating expenses. This does not mean that humans cannot or will not be able to monitor the results and adjust as needed. In fact, the law of unintended consequences ensures that a human should be monitoring for undesirable situations that would not normally be foreseeable. But the point of this is removing persons from the rote, repetitive tasks and allowing them to instead perform high-value work that is not well-suited for automation.

The aforementioned best practice approaches can be implemented piecemeal by connecting and integrating component solutions (for example, Skupper, `https://skupper.io/index.html` or OpenZiti, `https://openziti.io/`), in a cohesive solution or platform (for example, IBM Hybrid Cloud Mesh, `https://www.ibm.com/products/hybrid-cloud-mesh`, or Nephio, `https://github.com/nephio-project`), or as part of a platform engineering solution (for example, Azure Radius platform engineering, `https://github.com/radius-project/radius`).

With the preceding best practices in mind, let's discuss compatible approaches to security in edge-native application development, deployment, and operations.

Zero Trust or as close as you can get

In this section, we will discuss common and emerging practices to secure the application's use of the network, and what really matters. We will review major aspects of a Zero Trust architecture in the context of edge computing. By the end, you will be able to describe the approaches, what potential benefits they bring, and when they might be useful to your edge architectures.

Let's begin with the basics and discuss handling secrets. It can be surprising how often this discipline is overlooked or ignored, yet proper implementation is critical to prevent unauthorized access.

Managing secrets on the edge

Software development teams should not only be trained in how to securely connect applications to remote services but they should also be provided with edge-native solutions to enable them to properly manage the credentials, API keys, certificates, and other secrets. While some tools such as GitHub provide built-in secrets management capabilities, solutions that span the architecture should have a dedicated secrets management solution, such as Hashicorp Vault, EnvKey, or OpenBao.

While it is important to store secrets in a central location, it is also critical that administrators are able to do the following:

- Distribute secrets only to the applications that need them

- Send secrets only when they are needed

- Configure the secrets to be readable only by the intended applications

- Deploy, update/renew, and rotate certificates on demand

Do not embed secrets, credentials, or keys inside applications, containers, or even environment variables. Passing secrets as arguments on the command line is also not secure. Use a secrets management solution that stores the information securely and separately and only binds the secrets to the application at runtime.

Now that this topic has been addressed, let's step back and ensure familiarity with terms and principles for security in edge architectures, beginning with Zero Trust.

Zero Trust architectures in edge computing

The **Zero Trust Architecture (ZTA)** for remote, cloud-based assets published by NIST in SP 800-207 is shown in *Figure 9.2*. In the middle are the three core components:

- Policy Engine
- Policy Administrator
- Policy Enforcement Point

On the outside are the data sources providing input and policy rules to the core components.

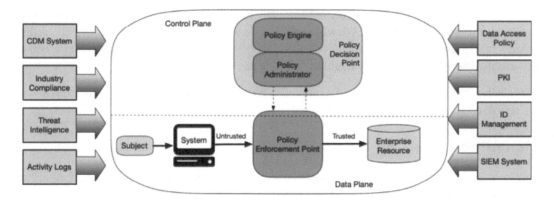

Figure 9.2 – ZTA from NIST

(*Image Source*: NIST SP 800-207: `https://nvlpubs.nist.gov/nistpubs/SpecialPublications/NIST.SP.800-207.pdf`.)

ZTA uses zero-trust principles when it comes to enterprise infrastructure and workflows, meaning no implicit trust is granted to any assets, devices, or user accounts, no matter where they are located or who owns them.

A common framework for implementing these zero trust principles in hybrid cloud and edge computing is the secure access service edge framework. Let's delve into that next.

Secure access service edge

There are unique security challenges with edge and distributed computing applications. The **secure access service edge** (**SASE**) framework addresses those challenges by combining Zero Trust security with wide-area networking. Hyperscalers offer SASE as a service applicable directly to edge devices, thus allowing devices and systems to securely connect to applications and services anywhere.

Instead of the traditional security perimeter around a data center, SASE offers policy-based security services at the edge. This is made possible by using a **software-defined wide area network** (**SD-WAN**) capability in the overlay network. Using SD-WAN lets enterprises scale their security posture. *Figure 9.3* shows the convergence of network and security services in a cloud-based SASE architecture:

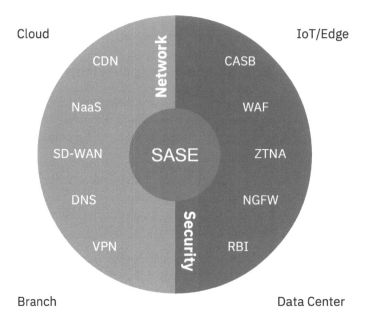

Figure 9.3 – The SASE architecture

The following are the descriptions of the technologies mentioned in *Figure 9.3*:

SASE – Secure Access Service Edge			
Network		**Security**	
CDN	Content Delivery Network	CASB	Cloud Access Security Broker
NaaS	Network as a Service	WAF	Web Application Firewall
SD-WAN	Software-Defined Wide Area Network	ZTNA	Zero Trust Network Access
DNS	Domain Name System	NGFW	Next Generation Firewall
VPN	Virtual Private Network	RBI	Remote Browser Isolation

Figure 9.4 – Glossary of terms

The policy-based approach that SASE provides is yet another example of the use of the declarative approach to application architecture configuration. Please note that it is largely focused on the network overlay. This is a good time to look at the network overlay and discuss how edge computing and application-centered networking should focus on this abstraction. Let's discuss how we should approach the overlay and underlay differently and the reasons for those differences.

Overlay, underlay, and shared responsibilities

Should edge computing architectures care about the underlying physical infrastructure, or should architectures just assume that the underlay exists, has standard capabilities, meets industry norms regarding **service-level agreements** (**SLAs**), and is reasonably well-maintained, and then abstract away any details and differences?

Enterprises can continue to use network segmentation, which is an architectural approach to isolate the internal network from the rest of the internet. In so doing, it not only improves security and access control but also helps with performance by creating access policies that are enforced via firewalls. With newer technologies now, there are other options.

In this section, we cover different approaches to edge-friendly network overlay implementations. Along the way, we discuss how the overlay can assist with network-level application isolation and why that is important. By the end, solution architects should be thinking about approaches to connect applications and services to each other and to cloud infrastructure.

The network underlay

In the *Industrial edge scenario* section in *Chapter 5*, we discussed the network underlay as a choice between public 5G and private 5G. In the *Retail edge scenario* section, we further discussed using network slicing for specific locations and use cases. Both of those are good examples of possible network underlay approaches. In commercial and residential deployments, various combinations of Ethernet and Wi-Fi are typically used for **local area networks** (**LANs**) in conjunction with repeaters as needed to extend coverage and prevent dead spots. In agriculture and other outdoor deployments, they may use a combination of LoRaWAN, Wi-Fi, and Bluetooth, or all three in a shared mesh.

However, these approaches potentially expose machines, hosts, and applications to each other and could allow traffic from one to interfere with traffic from others, in addition to traffic from other connected networks and the internet. To isolate one network or subnet from another, and to limit what traffic can pass between them, firewalls are typically used. However, this introduces configuration and maintenance overhead and can potentially block communications, which prevents distributed applications from functioning unless exceptions are introduced in firewall rules (which provides another potential attack vector). But what if machines did not open inbound ports for requests, and what if applications were not directly reachable by external sources?

The network overlay

Chapter 4 briefly described both the network underlay and the network overlay (which is the virtual network layer on top of the physical network infrastructure). The virtual aspect of an overlay allows the network to connect to thousands of edge devices quickly without needing to interact directly with physical network components. Devices on overlay networks are interconnected via logical links, making up the overlay topology. It is important to note that overlay network topology will vary based on the underlay network architecture.

By extending *Figure 4.3*, we see that edge devices can communicate directly with the networking components in the overlay, rather than overload the physical components in the underlay (see *Figure 9.5*). Another advantage of an overlay network is that because it is software-defined, it scales well.

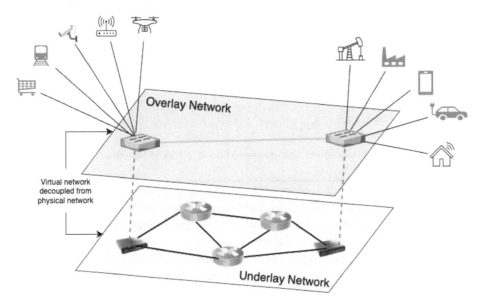

Figure 9.5 – Edge devices connecting to network overlay

With the distinctions between the network overlay and underlay explained, let's revisit Zero Trust in light of each.

Zero Trust Network Access

Zero Trust Network Access (**ZTNA**) is an emerging approach that authenticates users and devices, authorizes their secure access to each resource independently (other users, devices, services, applications, and infrastructure), and validates that access on a periodic and continuous basis. Like most Zero Trust approaches, it uses the principle of least privilege and defaults to denying all access before authorizing the context of the specific request. See *Figure 9.6*, which shows how ZTNA relates to the various actions and participants:

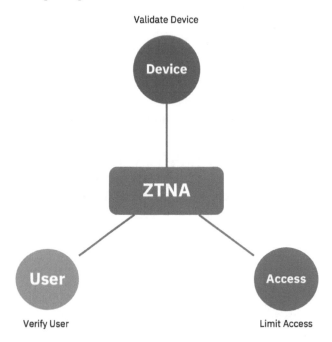

Figure 9.6 – ZTNA in edge computing and how it relates to system components

The ZTNA approach is well-suited to an edge computing solution because it provides a single, general-purpose solution for the wide range of heterogeneous edge devices that cannot be trusted but are generating and sending data to edge hubs. Since these edge devices cannot be locked in a secure location, it makes sense to enable access control policies on the edge devices and set up security policies at a more "central" location. A goal is to remove the implicit trust of those edge devices. While network teams bear responsibility for configuring elements in a zero-trust network, they should work closely with security teams to develop the overall ZTA. Incidentally, ZTNA 2.0 offers continuous trust verification of the devices and protects all data.

While there are many benefits to using ZTNA, it is not a complete security solution for edge networking. Solution architects must take a holistic approach and recommend SASE, which helps bring security services to WAN topologies such as those in edge computing.

After ensuring that all component services and users are connected and communicating with each other, it is critical to also confirm that only the intended participants in the conversation can read the messages being sent.

End-to-end encryption

When we talk about connecting, the next most obvious question turns to security. Enterprises always want to know whether the connection is secure. That is because a secure connection guarantees that the data flowing through that connection is encrypted, thus protected from promiscuous viewing by others on the same network segment. The connection can span many network hops, which are points or segments in the network along with data is passed.

End-to-end encryption (E2EE) means that the data is encrypted at the source and remains encrypted in transit until it reaches the intended destination. To put this in an edge computing context, the data generated by the edge device is immediately encrypted and transmitted over a secure network to the edge hub or even to the cloud, where, depending on the need and the application, it could be decrypted and acted upon or stored in the encrypted state. This requires an encryption algorithm at the source and a corresponding decryption facility at the destination before the data can be used. See *Figure 9.7*, which illustrates a hypothetical flow in an end-to-end physical solution:

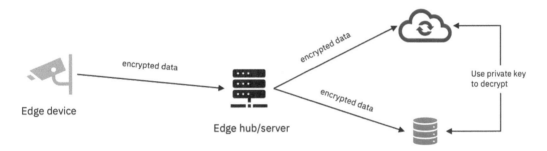

Figure 9.7 – E2EE in edge computing

Remember, E2EE ensures that only the sender and the receiver can see the data in its unencrypted form. There is no entity in the middle, such as the cloud provider or network operator, that can see the data using any kind of key. While encryption comes with a minor cost and inconvenience, sending unencrypted data over an unsecured network can be far more dangerous and expensive. Solution architects have to weigh up those factors while determining when and where encryption should be enforced, especially E2EE.

> **Note**
>
> Gartner defines encryption in the context of network-based communications as *"the process of systematically encoding a bit stream before transmission so that an unauthorized party cannot decipher it"* (`https://www.gartner.com/en/information-technology/glossary/encryption`).

To connect the concepts of known and authorized participants with the goal of ensuring that only those parties can read the messages being sent, let's add the concept of application isolation in a distributed solution.

Application-centric networking

Dynamically creating and managing network connections between applications, microservices, and infrastructure is a new capability provided by modern software networking solutions, which some have described as **application-centric networking** (**ACN**). Furthermore, the most comprehensive ACN solutions support endpoints from hyperscalers and cloud-based SaaS offerings, as well as enterprise, regional, and edge clouds, thus providing **hybrid**, **multi-cloud** application-centric network overlay connectivity in an application-centric model.

ACN first and foremost requires understanding the application's connectivity requirements in the form of the following:

- What it needs to connect to – local or remote services and infrastructure
- How it needs to connect – protocols and ports
- Prioritized performance targets – latency limits and response times

Then, it needs to understand the current network overlay and underlay topology and utilization and to be able to construct a model of that state. It also should understand the available deployment endpoint locations: providers, namespaces, cost, performance, and access methods. Lastly, it should have the ability to both observe the performance aspects of all of those in near real time and to deploy infrastructure in the form of gateways at each endpoint location and waypoint gateways at network interconnect points.

With the aforementioned capabilities, especially if they are integrated and can operate autonomously, a distributed application can react to changing network conditions and dynamically redeploy services from one endpoint location to another with no downtime. This is the promise of ACN for edge-based applications accessing remote resources in hybrid, multi-cloud endpoints.

Summary

In this chapter, we discussed how an application-centric approach to connectivity could increase application deployment velocity by orders of magnitude, thus enabling freedom of movement for applications, services, and software-based infrastructure. Furthermore, if this approach is implemented with a tool using declarative configuration and autonomous implementation, frictionless and reactive application component movement is possible in minutes instead of hours or days.

We covered security frameworks and paradigms that have recently emerged to handle zero-trust scenarios. These standards ensure that all connected components and systems are proactively identified and authorized for granular access.

We also covered the benefits of decoupling edge applications from the network underlay through an overlay abstraction. This allows application isolation from other network users and systems. Consider using approaches provided by application-centric multi-cloud networking connectivity or platform engineering solutions. These new and emerging practices will give your edge architectures the flexibility needed to rapidly adapt to changing environments while maintaining a secure posture.

In the next chapter, we'll discuss how enterprises can implement the newest software solutions in open source projects. We'll show how companies can contribute to these projects to ensure their needs and requirements are met without giving up intellectual property. We'll also cover how open source licenses can be abused, and how to protect your company from that risk.

10

Open Source Software Can Benefit You

Modern enterprise applications are typically 76% based on open source software (`https://www.synopsys.com/software-integrity/resources/analyst-reports/open-source-security-risk-analysis.html`). This chapter discusses strategies to ensure that these dependencies don't become your Achilles heel. Several recent well-publicized events have shown how companies that do not actively and continuously embrace open source principles can cause issues for those who depend on the software they maintain. In this chapter, we will discuss how mature open source software projects with open governance can attract more resources to your product development efforts and act as a force multiplier.

In this chapter, we will cover the following main topics:

- Open source and edge computing – the benefits and trade-offs
- SBOMs are your friend – securing the software supply chain with a Software Bill of Materials
- What makes you so special? Contribute without giving up intellectual property
- Let the cat out of the bag – successfully open source your code and documentation

By the end of this chapter, you will have learned how you can consume open source software while avoiding potential pitfalls. You will also read how enterprises have successfully contributed software to open source projects without giving up their intellectual property rights.

Suggested pre-reading material

- *Why do enterprises use and contribute to open source software* by Dan Whiting (`https://www.linuxfoundation.org/blog/blog/why-do-enterprises-use-and-contribute-to-open-source-software`)
- *Creating an open source program office* (`https://ospo-alliance.org/ggi/introduction/`)

- *OSPO 101 training* (`https://github.com/todogroup/ospo-career-path/tree/main/OSPO-101`)
- *Open Source Initiative approved licenses* (`https://opensource.org/licenses/`)
- *SPDX license identifiers* (`https://fossa.com/blog/understanding-using-spdx-license-identifiers-license-expressions/`)
- *Developer Certificate of Origin* (`https://developercertificate.org/`)

Open source and edge computing

In this section, we'll go over the benefits and trade-offs for companies relying on **open source software (OSS)** projects to supplement, support, and standardize their software product development process. You'll learn about how to build support in your company to use and contribute to open source foundations, and you'll become an advocate for this decades-old approach to collaborative endeavor.

Edge computing and OSS are intertwined

Edge computing, as it is now implemented, first began in earnest in late 2015 as an outgrowth of cloud computing (see `https://dzone.com/articles/a-brief-history-of-edge`) and so is much younger than open source software development. However, it began to hit critical mass in late 2018, just as the Linux Foundation began organizing its hundreds of open source projects into themed umbrella groups around natural affinities (meaning, categories naturally organized around a shared industry, technology, or market). Thus, LF Edge began in January 2019 with two mature projects and several new code contributions, and the Eclipse Foundation followed suit with its Edge Native Working Group. This meant that by the time that edge computing began to enter the public consciousness, a vibrant group of open source communities already existed as a nucleus to form standards around and to house blueprints for end-to-end solutions.

Edge computing, therefore, became the first modern open source native field in computing. The first software solutions were all developed as open source projects, and then commercially supported solutions downstream from those were created. Thus, the roots of edge computing are firmly grounded in OSS, and any changes or innovations in OSS will have a correspondingly large effect on edge computing as a whole.

Let's take a look at how this heritage of open source affects your software development velocity and overall effort and costs.

Do you really need to create that component?

The first OSS projects contributed to LF Edge revolved around utility-type component solutions that solved recurring problems and replaced large chunks of boilerplate code. They also implemented an edge-native approach to problem solving, unlike the **IoT** (**Internet of Things**) solutions from the previous 5–10 years that were all in the process of being converted to **SaaS**-based products. This points to the first major benefit of relying on OSS – you don't write and maintain code that is not your company's core competency and is not part of your product's value proposition. This adheres to the **don't repeat yourself (DRY)** principle and the *"don't re-invent the wheel"* idiom.

> **Something to think about**
> *Only create software components that implement your product's core value proposition.*

If a problem has already been solved, the solution has several adopters already using it in production, and it largely meets your needs, then how does it benefit you to invest the time and effort in attempting to solve the same problem yourself in isolation?

- The first instinct of a solution architect should always be to look for an existing component to reuse. Therefore, the first benefit of using open-source software solutions is that it provides a rich vein of re-usable solutions and components.

- The second major benefit of relying on OSS is being able to create solutions quickly through judicious re-use of existing components. Since re-using code is quicker than writing it from scratch, your project should take less time to write and debug, resulting in better code quality. This assumes that the code you re-use already has unit tests and complete code coverage, supports your coding standards, and its integration requires minimal effort.

- A third benefit of relying on OSS is that your code will inherit support for de facto and/or actual standards and conventions. The pattern that has emerged over the last few decades of software development is for a developer or tool to implement an approach, which is then for refined and improved, and then competing approaches emerge and either gain support from users of the previous approach or fail to gain significant traction, thus reinforcing support for the existing approach. Over time, the existing approach becomes the de facto standard, and it may even have the unique distinctives of the solution codified into an actual standard. We'd argue that any existing open source project that is being used in production by several products or companies has become a de facto standard.

- A fourth benefit of relying on OSS is that your product will be easier to maintain and have a shallower learning curve for new developers being onboarded the more you reuse existing OSS components. In many situations, developers may be familiar with existing standards and the libraries or components that implement them. Further, there will be an existing body of work (e.g., tutorials, videos, example code, IDE hinting, and autocomplete) available that demonstrates and documents how to use those components, and they will likely have been refined to follow familiar conventions and paradigms, which allow them to *converge on the familiar (meaning, this process is likely to produce a solution that will look familiar to architects and developers when they examine the details for the first time, therefore making it intuitive to understand and thus easier to maintain).*

- A fifth benefit of developing software and features as open source is that the burden, risk, and benefits of non-differentiating code and functionality can be shared between partners and even between competitors. This resource sharing lowers costs and, thus, also frees up resources to be better used elsewhere.

- Finally, a sixth benefit of relying on OSS is that support for those components can be outsourced, thus creating a smaller support burden for your product organization. This may take the form of referencing existing (external) documentation for those component features, contracting with an organization that provides commercial support for those components, or integrating existing external documentation into your product documentation if the source code and artifacts feature a license that allows this reuse.

Given the benefits outlined here, most organizations will experience more than a net positive experience if they leverage existing OSS components in their software development process. This leads to the next question – how can software architects encourage a culture of open source reuse within an enterprise?

Creating and supporting an open source program office (OSPO)

Later in this chapter, we'll cover consuming OSS without introducing new vulnerabilities, as well as contributing to OSS projects while retaining control of your intellectual property. In the meantime, let's go over the benefits of having a dedicated group in your organization tasked with the responsibility for promoting, influencing, and advising on the best approaches to consume from, and contribute to, OSS.

Your company or organization's interaction with OSS will be a net positive if, at minimum, there is a defined open source strategy. This strategy should address what consumption is allowed (and why), what contributions are allowed, how these align with the business and product strategy, and how to calculate and achieve a **return on investment** (**ROI**). An OSPO should manage and implement that strategy, either directly or indirectly, through delegation to groups in each business unit.

The TODO Group defines the role of an OSPO as follows:

"An open source program office is designed to be the center of the universe for a company's open source operations and structure, helping to bring all the needed components together. This can include setting code use, distribution, selection, auditing and other policies, as well as training developers, ensuring legal compliance and promoting and building community engagement. The office can also provide advocacy and communications about all things open source inside and outside the company." (`https://todogroup.org/zh-cn/resources/guides/how-to-create-an-open-source-program-office/`)

Let's look at an example of how this is implemented in a large enterprise today. Inside IBM's **CIO** (**Chief Information Officer**) office, the Open Technology team functions as an OSPO. They are responsible for managing annual developer training (which is required for all open source contributions), tracking developer contributions, and maintaining company-level agreements with open source foundations. The team gives talks both externally and within the company and has both developer advocates and project leaders active in many open source projects. They identify and track consumption of open source software across the company, facilitate collection and reporting on the software supply chain, including SBOM creation and usage, track and report on vulnerabilities, and ensure license compliance through regular code scans. They also maintain a short list of open source projects of strategic importance to the company and direct company-level investment in them.

Company divisions and units can also create their own open source or open technology strategies and align with a company-level strategy. Finally, larger umbrella organizations within foundations may have corresponding steering committees within a company to collaborate and coordinate on a unified, cross-unit approach to working within, and supporting, projects based on open-source software and technologies (`https://blog.opensource.org/the-five-stages-of-the-open-source-program-office/`).

As you can see in the preceding example, overall guidance is provided from a central group implementing the corporate open source strategy, while divisions and units have the flexibility to determine the specifics and align those with their business objectives. This approach enables standardized company-wide safe consumption of open source solutions. With a central team providing tools such as code scanning, coupled with individual units providing dependency graphs in the form of a software bill of materials, vulnerabilities can be quickly identified across an enterprise. Let's explore how this is possible in the next section.

A software bill of materials is your friend

In this section, we will explore OSS supply chain issues – how to consume or depend on OSS without introducing new vulnerabilities using a **Software Bill of Materials** (**SBOM**), how to identify mature and stable OSS projects, how to nurture and assist projects you rely on, and responding to projects that abandon their initial commitments.

Using SBOMs to track software dependencies

A software architect can be called on to provide specific recommendations for OSS solutions in an architecture or implementation. The risks in doing so are that the proper solution (or one of its immediate dependencies) for a given set of requirements might be from a project that is not mature or stable (see the following subsection for more about that topic). Therefore, it is incumbent on you to perform due diligence, either recommending against using those projects or only with strong caveats when no other good options are available, so that the ultimate decision-makers can make an accurate and informed determination.

Here are some tasks you should perform in order to analyze a set of dependencies for potential areas of vulnerability. This list should be considered the minimum due diligence, not an exhaustive set of steps. Think about how you might expand the following list below to cover your circumstances or unique situation:

1. The first step in performing an analysis of an OSS project's release is to obtain the SBOM files for both the source code and the released assets. It is critical to use both because code will rely

on different dependencies at build time compared to runtime. The project may make SBOMs available for their source code in GitHub repositories. See *Figure 10.1* for an example of where to look. Likewise, an SBOM can be easily generated from a container using Docker's CLI.

Figure 10.1 – A GitHub repository screenshot showing the Export SBOM function

2. The second step would be to review the SBOM contents, looking for critical, unaddressed vulnerabilities more than 60 days old. If you find any, it could mean that the project code is not maintained per the recommended standards from the **OpenSSF (Open Source Security Foundation)** if the associated **CVE (Common Vulnerabilities and Exposures notice)** is legitimately filed and properly describes a critical vulnerability that directly affects how code is used in this situation.

3. The third step would be to look at the licenses of the immediate dependencies to ensure that they meet your needs and requirements. This should include defining which licenses are compatible with the parent project, ensuring that only compatible licenses are used by dependencies and in contributions. A recommended resource to consult, if you have any questions about a software license, is the **Open Source Initiative's (OSI's)** list of OSI Approved Licenses at `https://opensource.org/licenses/`.

4. Finally, a fourth step would be to manually review the list of projects and repositories to see whether any of them have appeared in the news recently or on a trusted technology site, regarding any upcoming changes in license, unaddressed breaches or vulnerabilities, or community controversy or instability. If any of those names trigger a red flag or give you pause, consider investigating it more fully.

> **Note**
>
> At the time of writing, the authors were not aware of a tool that could automate all steps of the scan process outlined previously, but keep in mind that new tools may have been created or released since then.

Let others share your load

As you consider all of the work that needs to be done managing source code contributions and dependencies, keep in mind that organizations exist that will assist you with these tasks. Open source foundations such as the Eclipse Foundation, the Apache Foundation, and the Linux Foundation perform some or most of the preceding steps on behalf of developers, or may provide the tools needed to do so. For example, the Eclipse Foundation's **Intellectual Property** (**IP**) team will perform dependency license checks when accepting and onboarding a new project, and before accepting sizable contributions to existing projects. Also, these tools and services provided by the foundations are one element in a more comprehensive approach to managing cyber risk (`https://www.eclipse.org/org/workinggroups/eclipse-cyber-risk-concept.php`).

Now that we've reviewed code quality and risk management, let's look more closely at how to gauge an OSS project's overall maturity and how that relates to code quality.

The characteristics of a mature OSS project

Another aspect of OSS solutions that a solution architect should evaluate before making recommendations is a project's maturity and stability. The risks of using software from a source that is not yet mature would be that the project could suddenly change direction by removing critical features, adding unneeded features that cause performance issues, stopping the maintenance of documentation, or ceasing development work entirely.

If a component of your solution were to become unreliable in this manner or otherwise unavailable, how quickly could you replace it, and at what cost? Let's see some questions you should ask about a project that may require deeper investigation, before potentially adopting it for your solution or product:

- How is a community defined, and how large and active is it? Some projects that offer their software under an open source license believe that allowing anyone to submit or comment on an issue constitutes community engagement. Others feel that providing a forum for software users to communicate (e.g., chat rooms, discussion channels, and documentation comments) is sufficient. However, allowing the public to communicate with you is not the same thing as a group of **empowered stakeholders** giving input into a product roadmap or contributing code, designs, artwork, and documentation freely to a project. Just talking about a project is not the same thing as contributing to it. We would argue that a community should be comprised of persons who not only *use* a project but also meaningfully *contribute* to it, with their contribution acknowledged.

- How many adopters are there, and how long have they been active (are they still using it)? An indicator of not only the health of a project but also its value is the number of persons or organizations who actively use the solution. If those users are tracked and are willing to be publicly identified as users, then that is a strong signal of the intrinsic value the solution brings.

- How many companies participate in the community? If a company is not only an adopter but also actively contributes in some way, that indicates that the company finds strategic value in the solution and finds that using the software brings more benefits than developing something similar in-house. It also indicates that those running the project welcome the participation of others. If companies use project software but do not contribute back, it's possible that they are prevented from doing so, not necessarily that they are unwilling to.

- How often and how regular are code releases? Is there a published feature roadmap? Can the community submit feature requests? If a project has regularly scheduled releases every six months or less, this is a good indicator of a stable project with a history of discipline and the ability to follow a schedule. If those releases are being documented with an artifact developed by the community, such as an architecture decision record or a feature request, so much the better. Also, if you can see a history of detailed release notes, their development and release processes are likely sufficiently mature.

- Is the project leadership composition vendor-neutral? Are there regular elections from the community, or are leaders appointed by a company or small cadre of "insiders"? A key indicator of potential trouble in a community is when it is known for having a single leader or small group of persons who control all the decisions. While having strong opinions on how a task should be performed, or what a specific outcome should be, is not an issue here, see whether there is a track record of community requests being consistently overruled or ignored. If so, this could become an issue.

- What is the quality and coverage of the documentation? Documentation is typically the least-enjoyed task for volunteers on a project, so if the documentation is thorough, up-to-date, clearly written, and complete, then the project is likely healthy and mature.

- Is there a good amount of unit tests available? What is the code coverage like? Can you fork the repo and run an end-to-end test without it failing? Failing tests can be a sign of code rot and insufficient attention or a lack of resources. However, this should not be a disqualifying consideration if you are willing to work to remediate this deficiency.

In summary, an immature project may lack a (complete) governance structure, with leadership positions filled with experienced staff, designated or identified replacement staff for critical roles, active community members from several organizations, and consistent contributions from people of varying abilities. Open governance, where meetings are held publicly and recordings/minutes are published, and where a community elects its project leadership and holds them accountable, prevents unstable communities and "benevolent dictators" from controlling a project.

Try to avoid using any software from an immature or unstable project, or even better, get involved and work to remedy any shortcomings. Here are some thoughts on how to do so effectively.

How to nurture and assist projects you rely on

More than just avoiding using software from unsustainable projects, your organization (and likely *you*) should identify which dependencies are strategic to your product or solution, and then actively contribute to the project that maintains those dependencies to ensure their ongoing success. This is especially true for emerging fields such as edge computing.

The most important step in supporting a project is to get formally involved in a community. This may mean reaching out to the leadership of a project, and the parent foundation if there is one, to let them know that your organization finds value in their project and your intention to begin using it in production (becoming a project adopter). As you interact in community events and meetings, find out what they need – attend meetings, read their issues and product roadmaps, email or message team or group leaders, and ask them about the challenges they face. Eventually, see how you can dedicate resources and persons to a project and earn your way into leadership positions by contributing code (becoming a committer), squashing bugs, and eventually, reviewing commits (becoming a maintainer).

Once your enterprise is established in a community, it's time to use your resources to improve project organization by amplifying what the community is already working on, and by helping out where it requires the most assistance. Research and find out how the community is funded, what its budget is, and how well it stays within that budget. See what other contributions organizations have made. Ask what initiatives the community wanted to tackle but couldn't, and work with it to address the initiatives that will bring mutual benefit.

Another area where you can bring value is by spreading the message of how a project has brought you and others value. Discuss publicly how the project has helped you – publish articles, videos, refer others to the project, and volunteer to teach others. Be a developer advocate. See whether you have connections in your social network that you could introduce to project leadership, especially in areas or verticals that they would like to expand their reach in.

One of the most neglected areas in OSS projects is test coverage. Offer to assist with testing code, testing steps in documentation, and submitting fixes and patches in the requested format. This will go a long way toward improving code quality and catching bugs before they are included in a release.

Finally, personally offer to join the leadership of the project, whether actively chairing a group or advising from a board position. These simple but effective steps don't all cost money, but they are welcome in OSS projects and can make a big difference in the health and stability of a project. They also act as a counter to pressures within a project to stray from the original mission statement, or ignore foundational promises, as we'll discuss next.

Responses to projects that stray from their mission

Over the last few years, and increasing in frequency over the last year, companies that started out monetizing a commercial offering downstream from an open source project that they founded have migrated the license of the previously open source code to a more restrictive source-available license. This action provoked emotional responses in those consuming the code, ranging from shock and surprise to feelings of betrayal. Yet the founders did not do anything illegal, and they were trying to preserve a business that they had created from the ground up. Conversely, they could not have built their projects without the wealth of open source dependencies that they rely on.

What responsibilities did the founders have toward those who consumed the open source code, whether an actual community or not? And what backup plans should the consuming parties have had in place for this eventuality? What follows is purely the opinion of the authors and does not constitute legal advice. Always consult with legal counsel before acting or publishing potentially defamatory statements.

First, talk to the founders rather than gossiping or spreading hearsay. It's possible that you misunderstood the situation or didn't hear the whole story. Reality can be more complicated than most of us imagine. Also, it's possible that the situation is resolvable. In many cases, it can be done in a manner not originally anticipated.

Second, determine whether the situation really needs addressing, or whether it can be simply ignored. If it cannot be ignored, then consider what actions can be taken in response, up to and including creating a fork of the project or establishing a competing project or alternative. Keep in mind that most forks or competition typically fail to reach their objectives. Reach out to others who may also be affected, and see whether you can collaborate on an alternative. If you cannot, then that likely means that creating an alternative is not a good option.

Frederic Desbiens, program manager for IoT and edge at the Eclipse Foundation, sums up the situation regarding companies that migrate the licenses of their projects away from open source in this way:

"As such, they are breaking the dynamics of the open source ecosystem to their own benefit. Can you imagine the OSS ecosystem ten years from now if the licenses for the Linux kernel, GCC, or even bash were changed in the same way? There is a lesson to be learned here. Organizations valuing a healthy open source ecosystem should contribute to projects where contributions are accepted without copyright assignation. For example, the Eclipse Contributor Agreement leaves copyrights with the individual or organization making the contribution. This makes license changes such as the one you describe much harder since they would require consent by all copyright holders."

After discussing the SBOM, the dependencies that arise from it, and how to evaluate those, let's now turn to the topic of when and whether to open source your own solutions, or components of it. We'll also discuss aspects of contributing code to external OSS projects.

What makes you so special? (Contributing without giving up intellectual property rights)In this section, we'll go over strategies for contributing to open source software projects. The focus will be on protecting your intellectual property and copyrights while enabling sharing and collaboration. What follows are the opinions of the authors and does not constitute legal advice. Always consult with legal counsel before contributing to open source.

Common objections

When the authors consult with teams and companies about an open source strategy for their edge computing solutions, one of the first objections that companies invariably raise is a concern about "giving away" their intellectual property or competitive advantages. The concern appears to be that placing their code in the open gives their competition insight into the "secret sauce" that gives their products a competitive advantage, and that others will now be able to easily replicate their success.

It is the authors' opinion that any innovation worth protection *should* have a patent disclosure filed in advance of code being contributed or committed. One of the key factors identifying an invention worthy of this protection is that the idea is easily discoverable, although innovative. By contributing code, you help fulfill the discoverability requirement. Thus, contributing code to an open source project may strengthen your company's case, not weaken it.

Recommendations for contributing code

Additionally, many successful companies have built thriving businesses around open source projects. Well-governed OSS foundations have led the way by providing all of the recommendations in the following list. These recommendations cover contributing code, documentation, machine learning models, and other assets to open source projects while minimizing potential risk to profitability and competitive advantage:

- Patent protections and corresponding open source licenses should be harmonized. You should communicate with your patent attorney when you file your disclosure(s) and ensure that they know that you may create and contribute open source artifacts that implement your invention(s), choosing an OSS license that allows usage to that effect.

- All contributed files should contain an appropriate copyright notice. This copyright may not be legally removed, although others may append their own copyright lines as they amend or add to the files.

- Different files may be covered by different licenses. For example, computer code may be covered by an Apache 2.0 license, while the documentation could be licensed under CC BY 4.0 International. Ultimately, you should use a **Software Package Data Exchange** (**SPDX**) license identifier or expression in all file headers.

- All contributions should be signed with a **Developer Certificate of Origin** (**DCO**) when committed. This ensures that the contributor claims that they created the code and that they submit it under the specified license.

- Every organization should have a **Contributor License Agreement** (**CLA**) with the organization they contribute code to. The CLA describes the terms of contributions and protects OSS projects from potential future legal issues. These could include claims that a contribution was not authorized for a specific purpose, or that the contributor was not authorized to make the contribution.

- Machine learning models are a special case, as you should be concerned not only with the license of the resulting model but also the provenance of the data used to train it. Training data should also be scrutinized for potential bias so that the resulting model does not unintentionally weigh or exclude relevant factors, thus invalidating the results.

The preceding guidelines are an overview of the issues, concerns, and recommendations around protecting your property while collaborating with others in the context of an OSS project. If your organization has an OSPO, they will likely have a more complete set of guidelines and processes for you to follow. Also, if you don't have an OSPO in your organization or enterprise, we hope you now see the need for one to be created. Finally, consider working with an established OSS foundation if it meets your needs and goals.

Now that we've discussed how to protect your ideas and inventions while collaborating, let's jump into the specifics of how to actually make the contributions.

Let the cat out of the bag (Successfully open source your code and documentation)

In this section, we'll discuss different methods and approaches to open sourcing your materials, from the bare minimum to standard and formal approaches. By the end, you should have a good idea of your options and the benefits of each one.

Each of the options listed in this section share some common assumptions. Chief among those assumptions is that each repository should explicitly call out (meaning, draw attention to or otherwise direct the reader to) the main or default license. Do not make code available publicly without specifying a software license. Other assumptions are that each repository lists the maintainers, contributors, security reporting process, ways to contribute, and adopters. Finally, each repository should contain a README file (meaning, a file literally named "README" that contains information that should be consulted first) and a pointer to any other documentation.

Five options for open sourcing

The first and simplest option is to place source code in a public repository. This allows an organization to make the code available without the overhead of creating a formal project or concerns about building a community. In some situations, this option allows a company to "test the waters" and see what happens as a tentative first step toward a more robust and formal approach. However, ultimately, this is not a sustainable approach longer-term.

A second option is to find an existing project compatible with the aims of your code and either contribute it wholesale to that project, or incubate your code as a sub-project under the watchful eyes and mature supervision of a parent project and community. This option can be a shortcut or quick way to build an existing community, test the resolve of the contributing organization toward building a sustainable project eventually, and safely create the internal structures and processes for your eventual project while the intended leadership learns the ropes.

A third option would be to find an open source foundation that your company can work with to assist with the legal, structural, marketing, and process issues of creating a new project from scratch. They can assist you with all of the work needed to form the project and get it started, including setting up meetings, mailing lists, presentation materials, trademarks, logos, press materials, and publicity. They may also have existing services, including repositories, registries, CI/CD tooling, and website hosting.

A fourth option would be to forgo the formality of creating a project and community while associating the code with your company, by hosting it in a company-affiliated repository. This gives people the confidence in knowing who backs the code and that you may likely have a vested interest in the code's longevity, ongoing maintenance, and support. However, there is also a degree of uncertainty, since there's no guarantee that the company won't eventually change the license or halt funding and development of the code, thus effectively abandoning it.

Out of all the options listed here, the second and third are approaches used by the modern open source movement and foundations, and they most closely match the open governance model. Consider the benefits and drawbacks that we have outlined here when determining which of the options may work best for you.

Next, let's briefly touch on the topic of what makes a good candidate for open source.

What to open source

The preceding sections lead straight to this question – what artifacts, solutions, or application source code should be released as public open source? Given the large number of existing OSS projects, software architects shouldn't advocate for releasing something new unless it is of potential value to others. Here's the authors' take on what may be of value and interest to others, listed in order from most valuable to least:

- **Most importantly, working and supported code that solves a problem**: This code should build successfully in all stated environments, provide test coverage, and at a minimum, instructions on how to use it.

- **Code snippets, utilities, and examples**: These may not build on their own but are designed to demonstrate a concept or approach to a solution. They are most helpful when accompanied by robust comments or documentation.

- **Pseudo-code, explanation, and documentation**: These are not technically source code but are artifacts that directly or indirectly teach concepts and the usage of code.

- **Raw data, lists and tables, processed and annotated data, and information**: These can be used to provide input, training, and functions as a source of transparent data publishing.

Conversely, what is not likely to provide value when released as open source are the following:

- **Code that is under active development and does not function as-is**: If it does not work, the code should either be in a private repo or not merged into the main branch. The expectation is that public code made available in a main branch should be capable of being built and run.

- **Broken projects that used to work but do not anymore**: Code rot happens when it is not actively maintained. Projects in this state should be archived or deleted if nobody can be recruited to maintain them. An exception to this would be for code of historical value, especially when the runtime environment is no longer available, but this should be clearly stated in documentation.

In summary, consider releasing open source functional code that offers a solution and runs independently, not pieces or parts of a solution or incomplete code that requires other unavailable pieces to run. Code should build and run in all supported environments and have automated passing tests with each release, which are ideally regular. Abandoned or untouched or no longer supported code should be archived. If you don't want to receive and answer emails about code, archive it.

Summary

In this chapter, you read about four key topics related to using open source software in the emerging field of edge computing. The first section talked about why open source is so important to edge computing and hybrid cloud development. We also discussed the potential benefits that using OSS brings to solutions, including increased development speed and agility, support for standards, shallower learning curves, and easier outsourcing of component development.

The second section discussed the software supply chain and how to manage it more easily with an SBOM. This gives you the ability to track dependencies, and it exposes additional information that could lead an architect to identifying potential risks in the projects supporting those dependencies.

The third section then covered reasons to open source company-developed solutions or components. You learned about ways to contribute safely without adding risk. Finally, the fourth section actually delved into how you can open source artifacts, and when you shouldn't.

If you're reading the book chronologically, you should by now have a holistic view of edge computing architectures and archetypes, system components, best practices, and software contributions and collaboration. That leaves a few remaining topics that function as a sort of connective tissue between those areas – how you can architect solutions to respond to worst-case scenarios, and how to make application architectures that become more resilient when unplanned situations present themselves. We'll cover these in the final chapter.

11

Recommendations and Best Practices

Once you've understood and internalized the concepts, terms, and patterns of edge computing, this chapter delves into the pitfalls that we've experienced and shows you how to avoid making the same mistakes. The three main areas we'll cover involve practices that have been developed specifically for the edge-native environment, how to think about designing solutions that don't easily break but actually improve when they encounter adverse circumstances, and what to do when things go awry.

In this chapter, we will cover the following main topics:

- Edge-native best practices as an outgrowth of cloud native

- Make antifragile applications

- When things go wrong

By the end of this chapter, you will have gained a new perspective on how to architect long-lived and resilient solutions for edge environments. You will understand how to put these recommendations and guidelines into practice. You should also be able to guide developers and line-of-business executives appropriately by explaining how these principles will improve the solution and thus make it easier and less expensive to maintain.

Suggested pre-reading material

- *Antifragile: Things That Gain from Disorder* by Nassim Nicholas Taleb

- *Edge-native development best practices*, IBM (`https://www.ibm.com/docs/en/eam/4.5?topic=clusters-edge-native-development-best-practices`)

- *Why Software is Eating The World* by Marc Andreessen (`https://genius.com/Marc-andreessen-why-software-is-eating-the-world-annotated`)

- The power of proactive repair by Addy Osmani (`https://www.linkedin.com/feed/update/urn:li:activity:7131581009191456768/`)

Edge-native best practices as an outgrowth of cloud native

Cloud-native development best practices were initially formed from the convergence of adoption of the agile development process, learning how to effectively utilize shared infrastructure, and service-oriented architecture (as well as software eating the world). However, not all best practices from the cloud apply to the edge. Specifically, partially and completely disconnected operations, heterogeneous hardware and software environments, and the potential mobility of edge devices forced edge pioneers to take a hard look at what was learned, discard the lessons that no longer applied, and adopt new lessons, culminating in edge-native development best practices.

In *Chapter 1*, we discussed the edge-native programming model, in the *Cloud out versus edge in* section. In this section, we'll dive into three areas where those fundamental assumptions affect how we architect solutions. We'll discuss how an inversion-of-a-central-control-plane approach can be a more secure method for deploying applications to the edge, learn about the concept of dynamic runtime dependency resolution, and weigh the relative advantages of application deployment models.

Pulling can be more secure than pushing

The cloud-native approach to managing distributed resources was created in an era of cheap and ubiquitous, homogenous cloud computing where resources seemed to scale almost infinitely and cost pennies to operate. The remote systems they were designed to control were heterogeneous in nature and typically resource constrained. This approach to centralized control is exemplified in the smart server/thin client pattern and more recently borne out in cloud-based IoT platform solutions and even web-based and SaaS solutions. For a deeper dive into this topic, see the *Legacy IoT architecture* section in *Chapter 3*.

Centralized control operation can present both a security and a management challenge that distributed or decentralized control does not have. Here is a list of key differences and distinctions between the two:

- First, a centralized "directory" of all of the devices must be maintained, including storing credentials for each endpoint, updating them when their addresses change, and periodically rotating credentials. A process must be created and maintained for adding new endpoints and removing retired or re-imaged endpoints.

- Second, each endpoint would have to be listening for an inbound request from the central control solution, which requires an open port and a network route between the control plane and the endpoint. This adds network management overhead and complexity. Also, the open port on each endpoint opens up a potential attack vector for malicious actors.

- Third, if one exists between the control plane and the endpoint, it likely requires configuring those ports and connections on a firewall. As illustrated in *Figures 5.7* and *5.8*, that firewall likely exists and will need ports opened.

Collectively, this is a lot of maintenance overhead to create and manage information about each endpoint in at least three separate locations: on the endpoint itself, in the control plane solution, and a firewall, with potential custom network routing rules as well. Likely, the creation and maintenance of that information will involve more than one team and is not an automated or automatable process.

This centralized approach to control has been what IT staff have been traditionally used to. Still, we are fast approaching the point where edge-based solutions are less expensive to operate and are automatable. This is causing enterprises to consider re-patriating workloads and subsequently distributing them out to the edge where and when it makes sense.

The newer edge-native approach has been driven by the increasing ubiquity and lower costs of powerful and energy-efficient programmable compute resources available in the field and outside the four walls of traditional data centers. This compute, when coupled with cloud-native development tools and best practices, has enabled new paradigms of distributed control, especially when combined with autonomous solutions and potentially augmented with ML-based intelligence.

Distributed or decentralized control spreads the responsibility out toward the systems that need to take action, thus allowing secure and automated approaches to onboarding and managing edge endpoints.

To contrast this with the centralized approach of edge endpoint management, endpoints in a distributed, pull-based design only need to be authenticated with the control plane and authorized to use it, which means that no remote systems need to initiate connections to the edge node, nor do they need a login account. You can enable an edge node's access to a centralized control plane by an exchange of keys, thus eliminating the need for the creation of a centralized directory of devices and IP addresses or hostnames.

> **Note**
> Even with the decentralized, pull-based approach, you may want to consider adding an out-of-band management channel to provide remote access for troubleshooting purposes.

In the pull-based approach, the endpoints do not need an open inbound port, since all communication can be initiated by the endpoint, and thus will be indistinguishable from "normal" network requests, which are already likely to be configured and allowed on both the device and any intervening firewalls. Thus, no new configurations would need to be created and maintained in this arrangement.

To summarize, pulling eliminates the need to maintain a central directory of endpoints and credentials, removes the security risk of having open inbound ports, and enables automation of the configuration and deployment process by not requiring new network routing rules.

Now that you've seen how the edge-native, distributed approach to endpoint management simplifies and secures the deployments, let's take a look at how it can also simplify application dependency management as well.

Application dependency resolution approaches

When an edge computing node receives information about a workload, that configuration information would include data about the service to be executed as well as its dependencies. In order to properly initialize and execute the services, they must be started in the proper sequence successfully, thus requiring a dependency management strategy involving both *when* to resolve those dependencies and *how* to resolve them.

Managing these dependencies can get incredibly complicated and be a maintenance nightmare (unless you have an automated dependency resolution function), and you need dynamic runtime dependency resolution so that killing or upgrading one dependency doesn't cause you to need to restart the whole application (even in loosely coupled and/or stateless applications).

Your goal should be to minimize dependencies that affect service availability to the maximum extent possible. Services should therefore be able to work in a disconnected or offline mode, which would allow them to accept requests even if other services they depend on are unreachable.

Managing the service software life cycle of containerized applications with dependencies is difficult, but managing them remotely without the ability to log on to the host is even more difficult. Let's begin by defining the stages of the life cycle of edge-native applications, shown in *Table 11.1*:

Stage	Description
Publishing/deployment	This is the act of transporting a container image binary or application package from a repository to the endpoint destination securely. This stage includes validating the application once it reaches the destination to ensure the artifacts match the expected characteristics. It should also include persisting the artifacts locally on the destination so that they remain available through host restarts.
Initialization/execution	This stage optionally includes deploying secrets and configuration, then starting the application. There may be separate parameters for the first execution compared to subsequent starts.
Operation (updating, monitoring, restarting, rollback, and inspecting)	The operation stage covers updating an application per configuration when a newer version becomes available, inspecting the running state, restarting if it terminates unexpectedly or the host restarts, and rolling back the application to a prior version per configuration.

Stopping/removal	This stage covers halting and optionally removing running services. It may include removing resource dependencies that are no longer in use or needed.

Table 11.1 – Edge-native application life cycle stages

With an understanding of the stages outlined in the previous table, let's explore how some tools infer service dependencies while others explicitly specify them and their relationships.

Implicit versus explicit dependency definitions

Some or all of the stages in the service software life cycle as depicted in the preceding table are typically managed directly on the host with tools such as Docker Compose, or in Kubernetes clusters with tools such as Helm charts. An important consideration to keep in mind is that these tools do not allow the definition of explicit service dependencies and that services are run at the execution stage in the order in which they are defined. In other words, they utilize an **implicit dependency approach**, meaning that the order in which services appear in the configuration *may* imply dependent relationships, but likely only indicate a preference in the order in which they should be initialized.

Other tools, such as Open Horizon, enable an agent running on the host or in a cluster to independently manage the service software life cycle. Open Horizon defines explicit service dependency relationships in service definition files. This allows each service's dependencies to be initialized and executed before the parent service regardless of the order in which they are defined. It uses an **explicit dependency approach**. An advantage of this approach is that service upgrades can be more granular and that the whole application does not necessarily need to be restarted if one service or dependency is updated or restarted.

Stateful versus stateless service considerations

A **stateful service** is one in which some or all of the required information used in a request is kept or otherwise persisted between successive invocations. A **stateless service**, on the other hand, sends all required information to service that request in that invocation.

When deploying applications that may have more than one dependency on a single stateful service, ensure that your tools do not duplicate the stateful service. For example, Open Horizon allows you to specify a dependency as a **singleton** to prevent multiple instantiations when multiple services share a single, stateful service dependency.

On the other hand, you may wish to run multiple instantiations of a single service if you need to upgrade one dependency pair independently of another, or for performance reasons if your environment is not resource constrained and you are load balancing between them in a high-availability architecture.

Deployment models for distributed edge applications compared

In the previous sub-section, we discussed application dependency management approaches, which assumed that the containerized application dependencies were being deployed to, and executed on, a single host. Now, in this sub-section, we'll investigate ways to deploy applications and their dependencies when they collectively span multiple hosts.

Tightly coupled microservices used in edge applications are ones in which resources are shared, interfaces are specific or dependent, or requests are synchronous. In these situations, the application should be treated as a monolith and both tested and released in a single deployment. This approach goes against the spirit of edge-native application development, but there are specific scenarios that may require it, usually involving stateful and transactional applications.

Loosely coupled microservices tend to be called asynchronously, encapsulate all dependencies internally, and do not introduce breaking changes outside of a major version update. These characteristics should allow individual services to be updated without scheduling application downtime, and without requiring an update to any other services.

As part of the deployment process, applications should have their performance characteristics compared to a previous baseline to ensure that they do not negatively impact their target deployment host environment or exceed available resources. For example, if a service previously utilized 30 MB of storage and 2 GB RAM, those requirements may have been added as deployment properties for the service and as availability constraints on the edge node. If the update requires more RAM, ensure that any policy properties and constraints have also been updated and that any assumptions about target device resource availability are still valid.

In all of the preceding discussions, the danger being avoided with the solution designs is creating applications that easily fail when operating, maintaining, and migrating. But is there an approach to creating edge architectures that can circumvent or mitigate the tendency toward frailty? More than being reactive and implementing self-healing, can we be proactive and prevent potential breakage in the first place? Let's explore this in the next section.

Making antifragile applications

In this section, let's explore how to design solutions that improve when placed under stress. We'll analyze potential areas of weakness. By the end of the section, you should be able to list some properties of an antifragile solution architecture. The goal of this section is to give you a new perspective and a new way of thinking about creating lasting and invulnerable applications, rather than delivering specific recipes for you to follow.

Defining the terms

What do we mean when we use the term **antifragile**? In Nassim Nicholas Taleb's book *Antifragile*, he describes systems that not only *endure* and *survive* adversity but *improve* under pressure and attacks. While not written specifically about designing resilient application architectures, the principles covered in his book apply generally to most systems, including those used in software, and that's how we'll be applying the lessons discovered and explained by Taleb.

Designing architectures for situational adversity and uncertainty that thrive under pressure ensures that your infrastructure and system components are strong from the start. And the reverse is also true: *designing for nominal circumstances ensures that your solution will likely buckle when placed under pressure.*

Building an approach that remains strong when introduced to adverse circumstances implies an awareness of where the stress will come from and how it may affect your solution and its components. This requires a holistic and detailed knowledge of the solution and potential deployment environments and creative thinking about how it could be used. As you think through these issues, we recommend creating a list of potential areas of vulnerability and sorting them by most concerning to least so that you can spend the most time working on the areas that need the most attention.

What are your current areas of weakness or vulnerability?

As you create your solution architecture, we recommend being transparent about the trade-offs you encounter. Detail the points where improvements could have been made and why they weren't. Work with the development and product organizations to ensure you all understand the strengths and weaknesses. You may be able to turn what you felt was a point of fragility into a product feature or selling point. Here are some specific areas of potential weakness to ponder when creating a solution design:

- **Connectivity**: As covered earlier, DDIL environments describe the range of potential connectivity effects, and an offline-first posture can remediate that. Think about the potential sources of connectivity loss or degradation and see how that might be mitigated or used as a feature.

- **Physical access**: This is a potential area of vulnerability, but also the primary method of access for provisioning devices and ongoing hardware maintenance. Moving to a system of zero-touch provisioning, onboarding, and life cycle management will partially offset the lack of access to the hardware. Strategies to quarantine potentially compromised devices, and to flag the data they produce as suspect, would help. How might people potentially abuse having physical access and can that be turned from a weakness into a strength?

- **Environmental factors**: Air quality, temperature extremes or volatility, and vibrations all contribute to decreased operating conditions and potentially rapid equipment failure. Are there negative operating modalities that have positive aspects you could leverage?

- **Peak demand**: Systems are typically provisioned for an anticipated range of demand or usage. What are the worst-case scenarios regarding short-term impacts? And what if a product that uses your system proves wildly successful and you need to scale up quickly for the long term?

- **Hardware or software dependencies**: Is your solution tied to a specific type of hardware, a software library from a specific vendor, or a proprietary connector or protocol? If you can't abstract away from or around that dependency, can you prevent it from becoming a **single point of failure (SPoF)**?

Once you've probed and documented areas of potential weakness in your solution architecture, it's time to think about what situations and features make an architecture antifragile. Dwell on the following properties and consider how they might apply to your situation. Use them as a test to determine whether your architecture is either fragile or antifragile.

Properties of antifragile architectures

Taleb stated that antifragility is measurable using a straightforward test of asymmetry. Let's think about how this would apply to a solution that you design. When subject to random events, does your solution as a whole deliver more positive benefits or more negative results? If, in the balance, the results are more positive, then your approach is likely antifragile.

Let's think about scoring antifragility in the context of **machine learning** (**ML**) models. Object recognition models are typically trained with large labeled datasets of imagery, and can then be used to score the likelihood that a previously unseen image is an object that it recognizes. These models are known for failing to recognize objects they were trained on when shown the target object from a different perspective, with a new background, or in a different color or lighting arrangement. Since it does not deliver a net benefit when exposed to novel or random inputs, it is quite fragile.

Another property of antifragile architecture is that it responds well in unpredictable environments and unanticipated situations. Another way to think about this property is how well your components, infrastructure, or solution respond to edge conditions and corner cases. If-then logic, most algorithms, and some types of ML work best with known inputs, situations, and sequences. Therefore, attempting to predict and capture most scenarios *in advance* and responding appropriately would lead to a antifragile implementation.

A counter-intuitive property of an antifragile solution design is that the system becomes inefficient or weaker overall if volatility is suppressed, minimized, or otherwise filtered. For example, polling for messages at a scheduled interval is a fragile design since it generates load on a server by repeatedly checking for messages in situations when there are no messages for an extended time period, and likewise causes a backup when there is a surge in messages over a short time period because it is not able to check for messages more frequently.

However, polling at a variable rate in combination with a back-off algorithm allows the system to handle surges whenever they occur, quickly drain a queue or backlog, and then return to a slower interval as the number of messages declines. This would be an antifragile approach.

Some system types and patterns are fragile by their very nature, including command and control and other complex systems. The main cause of this fragility is the high number of interconnections and interdependencies. These not only mask the causes of certain responses but also prevent simple debugging. Therefore, the best way to reduce fragility in these types of systems is to reduce the complexity of the solutions employed within them.

An ounce of prevention...

While the end goal of antifragility is to prevent situations that could introduce negative results and a lack of flexibility, it is also important to backstop that with functions or components that will also correct any errors or misconfigurations if they can be easily anticipated. This attempt at self-healing is also a valid secondary approach to antifragility in edge architecture. It can also function as a substitute for first-level technical support by implementing checks for, and corrections to, frequently encountered issues on day two (after the solution has launched and is in production).

Overall, being antifragile means delivering a way to remove disorder from a system, or otherwise increasing order. But no matter how well designed a system is, eventually major issues can and will happen. Let's take a look at how to respond in the final section of this chapter.

When things go wrong

In the previous section, we wrote about patterns that benefit from adverse events and unpredictability. But it is just as important to realize which patterns we should avoid, since they are fragile, prone to failure, inflexible, brittle, and temporal. In most of this book, the authors have sought to warn away from certain behaviors, structures, approaches, and implementations for these reasons. In this final section of the book, we will attempt to bring it all together into a series of steps to take to first avoid, and second to recover, from potential disasters and failures.

What to avoid

It can be beneficial to re-state the obvious at times. More experienced architects will just assume these fundamental axioms, and thus run the risk of not passing them on to more junior staff. Let's review the basics:

- **Always have a plan B**. That means that you should assume that code (or networks and systems) will fail at the most inconvenient moments and bake in functionality that uses the circumstances to your advantage.

- **Do not intentionally introduce errors**. You may have heard the oft-used phrase in agile programming *Fail fast, fail early*. Be careful with that thinking because it has unintended consequences. "Iteration while failing forward" is a better concept because it ensures that you catch small errors quickly and fix them as you progress. One of the funniest and saddest errors we ever saw was a log message stating *The code should never execute this function*.

- **Always test under load**. There will always be one or two scenarios you cannot anticipate until you thoroughly stress-test a solution. That holds true for edge computing architectures especially when you deploy to thousands or tens of thousands of heterogeneous edge devices across scores of disparate environments.

- **Do not make unvalidated assumptions**. All inputs, operating conditions, system requirements, bills of material, and outputs should be validated. If possible, the reasons for each should be documented to prevent the Chesterton's fence condition where nobody knows the reason why a feature or function exists and thus does not know whether it can be safely removed.

- **Requirements should be written with the end user's input**. It is imperative to work with your customer when performing acceptance testing of your solution. If you do not, you run the risk of either creating what was not requested or missing fundamental features.

Anti-patterns

What patterns are bad for your architecture? Identifying processes or patterns that are not helpful or are counterproductive is just as important as knowing which patterns to adopt.

By definition, an anti-pattern is an approach to solving a software engineering challenge that appears to be useful, but whose outcomes are ineffective or cause more problems in the long run when adopted. They are considered to be bad programming practices and should be avoided.

What situations expose anti-patterns?

The following points communicate the root causes that the authors have seen developers repeat. Therefore, we must assume that the lessons learned are non-intuitive or otherwise not obvious:

- **Attempting to scale an existing solution**: Your operations team might have a well-defined manual process for provisioning, deploying, and managing an edge resource. It may have been working well in an existing fleet comprising tens of devices. But that process might not scale well, and even become a bottleneck, when deploying to a larger fleet of hundreds or thousands of devices.

- **Applying a solution from one class to all classes**: All edge devices are not the same, so when it comes to deploying them, solution architects cannot treat them as a single monolithic group. You should consider categorizing them according to their purpose, product or vertical affinity, or innate properties before creating a solution for each group or class. Once all solutions have been considered, then propose any optimizations.

- **Using the same methods in all operating contexts**: In earlier chapters, we discussed the disconnected edge. Your edge solutions should not assume that all devices will be always connected to the network. Your designs should take into consideration that the edge devices will have to continue to operate in a disconnected mode. The duration of the disconnection is something that must be worked out between the architect and the customer.

How to recover, gracefully or not

There are times when technology goes wrong and it is hard to recover gracefully. At one point or another, we all have relied on the navigation system in our cars and ended up at an incorrect destination. The only recourse in that situation is to backtrack or contact a human who can help you. Similarly, in an edge computing solution, if an animal or nature somehow wreaks havoc on a field-deployed device, the only recourse might be to send a human to rectify that problem. While uncommon, one has to be mindful of such a worst-case scenario.

- **Follow the plan**

  The first step should be to follow your formal **disaster recovery** (**DR**) plans. More importantly, ensure that they are tested and you know that they work. Next, ensure that you test them on a scheduled basis by conducting drills. In the case of architectures utilizing high-availability or standby scenarios, ensure you alternate testing so that all permutations are eventually exercised. Also, ensure that the backup structure is kept intact, even when employees leave the organization.

  We often see a decal on fire extinguisher cabinets that reads *In case of emergency break glass*. What we don't know is whether the fire extinguisher will work when needed. In the same vein, when an edge hub goes down, will the newly disconnected edge devices continue to generate data? When the hub is replaced or brought back online, will everything sync up correctly? That's why having the best DR design in an architecture is not enough. It needs to be tested by simulating real-world situations. Only then can one be sure to recover from a real disaster.

- **What if there isn't a plan?**

  If there isn't a plan, we have two options:

  - Revert to the last known working state, even if that ultimately means rebuilding from scratch. It's always faster the second (or third) time. Then, re-apply subsequent changes while continually monitoring. In this way, you can iteratively restore functionality and return to the current state. Hopefully, you are following product requirements to ensure proper functionality. If those do not exist, document and create those requirements as you go.

  - If reverting and rebuilding from there does not work, triage and build from scratch, beginning with the most important function first. Try to use off-the-shelf solutions as much as possible.

- **Prevent issues from recurring**

  Here are some hard-won lessons we've learned from edge computing deployments that we've seen, heard about, or participated in. We hope that you will not repeat these same errors.

  Always have a plan B, even if not thoroughly thought through. *Make sure you know alternatives for infrastructure, providers, platforms, processes, solutions, optimizations, and personnel.* We used to joke about not knowing what we'd do if one of our leaders got hit by a bus, but that points out a very real issue. For example, each leader should have an identified backup person or alternate, even if it's only temporarily while that leader is off sick or on vacation. This helps ensure business continuity by ensuring that everyone knows "who has the D" (decision-making powers in a situation or circumstance) and also that no business-critical knowledge is solely vested in a single individual but instead everyone is cross-trained. Likewise, ensure that you've considered a backup or alternate provider, solution, device, or system component.

Given that, systems should be designed to prevent outages in the future at a minimum by having hot or warm backups or alternative processes and systems, *especially if the backups operate in a different modality than the primary systems they are designed to backstop*. One way to prevent future hiccups is to visualize existing data with the right tools to better identify possible weak links. While edge computing solutions are used in predictive analytics use cases, the same rigor needs to be applied to the edge solution architecture itself. That could be achieved by autonomic computing or a variant of self-analysis.

Don't expect a solution component to function in a substantially different manner, even when placed in a new context. This applies both to optimizing performance as well as attempting to mitigate poor results. When it comes to investment advice and picking stocks, we have all heard the phrase *past performance is not indicative of future results*. On the contrary, you can tell a lot from the past performance of machines and IT systems. You might not be able to predict exactly how physical components in an edge solution will work or interact with each other in a future use case or solution, but you *can* get a good understanding of how most of the software system components will operate in the near future based on their past performance characteristics.

But the ultimate points here are to observe operating characteristics, collect and analyze data, draw inferences about operating behavior, perform small tests to confirm your assumptions about the behavior, document and disseminate your learnings, and implement those as best practices throughout your systems. Also, on a scheduled, periodic basis, re-confirm your assumptions to ensure that the operating environments have not changed sufficiently to invalidate your practices. The salient point is that your systems will require constant, ongoing care. They should be thought of as living entities in the sense that they will slowly change and develop new quirks over time.

Summary

In this chapter, we detailed errors and mistakes that you might commonly encounter both in designing architectures and in working with existing deployed solutions. Some of the remedies we've reviewed may seem like common sense to you, but not to others.

We went over practices that were developed specifically for the edge-native environment: pulling versus pushing and their security implications, discussing application dependency management and resolution approaches, and deployment models. The next section covered ways to think about designing antifragile solutions that improve when placed under stress instead of breaking when exposed to random events. In the last section, we went over our options when systems fail.

As a result, you should have a list of considerations that will help you to architect long-lived and resilient solutions for edge environments. We hope that you will not only put these recommendations and guidelines into practice but also pass along what you've learned to both developers and management. And when you do, please mention where you read about them.

Index

Symbols

Packtpub.com

Subscribe to our online digital library for full access to over 7,000 books and videos, as well as industry leading tools to help you plan your personal development and advance your career. For more information, please visit our website.

Why subscribe?

- Spend less time learning and more time coding with practical eBooks and Videos from over 4,000 industry professionals

- Improve your learning with Skill Plans built especially for you

- Get a free eBook or video every month

- Fully searchable for easy access to vital information

- Copy and paste, print, and bookmark content

Did you know that Packt offers eBook versions of every book published, with PDF and ePub files available? You can upgrade to the eBook version at packtpub.com and as a print book customer, you are entitled to a discount on the eBook copy. Get in touch with us at customercare@packtpub.com for more details.

At www.packtpub.com, you can also read a collection of free technical articles, sign up for a range of free newsletters, and receive exclusive discounts and offers on Packt books and eBooks.

Other Books You May Enjoy

If you enjoyed this book, you may be interested in these other books by Packt:

Software Architect's Handbook

Joseph Ingeno

ISBN: 9781788624060

- Design software architectures using patterns and best practices
- Explore the different considerations for designing software architecture
- Discover what it takes to continuously improve as a software architect
- Create loosely coupled systems that can support change
- Understand DevOps and how it affects software architecture
- Integrate, refactor, and re-architect legacy applications

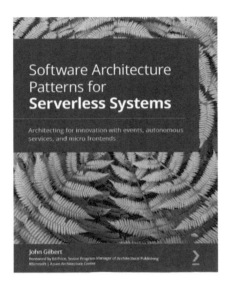

Software Architecture Patterns for Serverless Systems

John Gilbert

ISBN: 9781800207035

- Explore architectural patterns to create anti-fragile systems that thrive with change
- Focus on DevOps practices that empower self-sufficient, full-stack teams
- Build enterprise-scale serverless systems
- Apply microservices principles to the frontend
- Discover how SOLID principles apply to software and database architecture
- Create event stream processors that power the event sourcing and CQRS pattern
- Deploy a multi-regional system, including regional health checks, latency-based routing, and replication
- Explore the Strangler pattern for migrating legacy systems

Packt is searching for authors like you

If you're interested in becoming an author for Packt, please visit authors.packtpub.com and apply today. We have worked with thousands of developers and tech professionals, just like you, to help them share their insight with the global tech community. You can make a general application, apply for a specific hot topic that we are recruiting an author for, or submit your own idea.

Share Your Thoughts

Now you've finished *Edge Computing Patterns for Solution Architects*, we'd love to hear your thoughts! Scan the QR code below to go straight to the Amazon review page for this book and share your feedback or leave a review on the site that you purchased it from.

https://packt.link/r/1805124064

Your review is important to us and the tech community and will help us make sure we're delivering excellent quality content.

Download a free PDF copy of this book

Thanks for purchasing this book!

Do you like to read on the go but are unable to carry your print books everywhere?

Is your eBook purchase not compatible with the device of your choice?

Don't worry, now with every Packt book you get a DRM-free PDF version of that book at no cost.

Read anywhere, any place, on any device. Search, copy, and paste code from your favorite technical books directly into your application.

The perks don't stop there, you can get exclusive access to discounts, newsletters, and great free content in your inbox daily

Follow these simple steps to get the benefits:

1. Scan the QR code or visit the link below

https://packt.link/free-ebook/9781805124061

2. Submit your proof of purchase
3. That's it! We'll send your free PDF and other benefits to your email directly

Made in United States
Troutdale, OR
10/25/2024

24129442R00120